Supporting Language Learning in Everyday Life

School-Age Children Series

Series Editor
Nickola Wolf Nelson, Ph.D.

Supporting Language Learning in Everyday Life

Judith Felson Duchan, Ph.D.
State University of New York at Buffalo

SINGULAR PUBLISHING GROUP, INC.
SAN DIEGO, CALIFORNIA

Singular Publishing Group, Inc.
4284 41st Street
San Diego, California 92105-1197

© **1995 by Singular Publishing Group, Inc.**

Typeset in 10/12 Palatino by CFW Graphics
Printed in the United States of America by McNaughton & Gunn

Library of Congress Cataloging-in-Publication Data

Duchan, Judith F.
    Supporting language learning in everyday life / Judith F. Duchan
        p.   cm. — (School-age children series)
    Includes bibliographical references and index.
    ISBN 1-56593-221-8
    1. Language disorders in children.   2. Pragmatics.   I. Title.
    II. Series.
    RJ496.L35D83   1994
    618.92′655 — dc 20   94-29227
                                                          CIP

Contents

Foreword

C hildren learn language in situations. A "situation" implies a context that two or more participants share. The essence of a particular situation can be found in the shared purpose of the participants and the organization of the event. Child language specialists have examined a variety of communicative situations and have emphasized their importance for decades, particularly for toddlers and preschool-age children. Situations like "getting dressed," "eating lunch," or "playing house" have all been appreciated for their language-learning opportunities. With this background, it is a wonder that language specialists have taken so long to recognize similar opportunities for fostering language development in the situations of school-age children.

Not so, Judy Duchan. Over the years, I, like others, have been stimulated to think differently about all kinds of situations by the things Duchan has said and written. Thus , I was thrilled when she agreed to write this book. Duchan, of course, being Duchan, already had an outline clearly in mind for introducing readers to the potentials of "situated pragmatics." The cogent review of historical approaches to conceptualizing language intervention that readers will find in Chapter 1 was part of that plan. The historical perspective helps explain why language specialists have taken so long to appreciate the language-fostering opportunities of naturally occurring situations. Chapter 1 also introduces the earlier ideas of professionals from a variety of disciplines that are beginning to take root today.

In Chapter 2, Duchan leads readers to consider six different contexts (social, emotional, functional, physical, event, and discourse) that influence how individual language learners experience various situations. Subsequent chapters deepen this multifaceted view so that practitioners can conceptualize supports to address a child's complex contextual needs. In our traditional experience, speech-language pathologists use terms like "language intervention" to describe their attempts to assist children whose language acquisition does not proceed as expected. Duchan's characterization of this process as "support," rather than "intervention," helps us reconceptualize and normalize this process. It is also consistent with one of the themes of the School-Age Children Series which presents intervention as "fostering normal development."

Other themes of the School-Age Children Series are embodied in Duchan's book as well. The theme of collaboration is inherent in the process of working with others to design and implement plans for supporting children's language development. Change, both in children's abilities in certain situations, as well as change in contexts appropriate for children, are series themes that Duchan weaves throughout her book. It is a book that promises to help practitioners make sense of theory in practice, serving not as a how-to book, but — as Duchan notes in the Preface — a "how to think about what to do book." Most importantly, *Supporting Language Learning in Everyday Life* contributes to fulfilling the overriding purpose of the series — to support the provision of services that are relevant to the real-life needs of children.

Thus, it is with great satisfaction and pleasure that I introduce this fine book by Judith Felson Duchan. It is a major contribution to the School-Age Children Series, but more, to meeting children's needs. That is what makes it so fine.

Nickola Wolf Nelson, Ph.D.
Series Editor

Preface

A child reaches for an offered object. A teacher designs a question to fit a child's level of understanding and interest. An adult offers a child a phrase to use to ask for something. A cashier responds to a question typed by a customer using facilitated communication. First grade children in an included classroom pretend they are going grocery shopping. A father and son build something together.

The above events all involve communication and can offer children important insights about how to understand what is going on and to communicate meaningfully. They are all situations which are commonly carried out by members of different cultures, situations that are taken for granted and not usually seen as occasions of instruction.

The aim of this book is to develop in detail a type of language instruction based in such events. The approach has been called **situated pragmatics**, to contrast it with other, less-situated types of pragmatic intervention, such as those with goals of teaching children different "speech acts" or "turn taking" in different contexts. (See also Duchan, Hewitt, and Sonnenmeier [1994] for a comparison of pragmatics and situated pragmatics approaches.) The assumption of the less-situated programs has been that children can learn to carry out pragmatic acts such as requesting or getting and giving up the conversational floor and can readily transfer their new learnings to unfamiliar events without needing to know the ingredients of those new situations. Situated pragmatics includes an account of which sorts of events allow for, say, requests and what types of requests are appropriate in those situations; it also requires a consideration of how discourse is structured, and how the structure of discourse (and the event) influences pragmatic activities such as requesting.

The situated pragmatics view assumes that the process of understanding language is part and parcel of understanding the world. Further, it assumes that understanding the world involves more than looking out on it and remembering what what one sees. Rather than a mimetic or copy view of learning, the situated pragmatics view argued here is that children must interpret what is going on by inferring nonobservable meanings. To understand others' requests, one must infer from the context that individuals' behaviors and words indicate a request. To understand meanings behind the experiences of everyday events, one must infer the social roles and intents of individuals in those contexts as well as the temporal, spatial, and causal relationships between the parts of the experiences. The assumption, then, is that to understand events in the world one must do more than memorize and classify like events. A mental representation of what is going on involves a lot of relevant interpreting, or what we will be calling "sensemaking."

Finally, in the view of situated pragmatics, the clinical enterprise is to provide situational support to the potential learner. Adults and peers in the learning context knowingly or unknowingly provide the learner with support in a variety of ways and in a variety of domains or contexts. The support contexts selected for special focus in this book are: the social context, the emotional (affective) context, the functional (intentional) context, the physical context, the event context, and the discourse context.

Intervention support contexts are relevant for any child, whatever the particular goals of treatment. When provided with relevant support from these different context domains, the child can make better sense of and be more included in everyday life situations — the ultimate goal of any intervention program. Thus, while other intervention approaches emphasize how to target and teach what a child needs to learn, the emphasis here is on providing contextual support to make communication a successful and understandable experience. The enterprise is to support children who have difficulty communicating, however severe, so that they can become more included in the social and cultural mainstream.

The book is not a how-to book. Rather it is a how to think about what to do book. It takes issue with some of the prevailing perspectives governing our approaches to language intervention, such as behavioral and linguistic approaches, and even with some of the ways we think about what we do as language interventionists. For example, it makes the case that what we are trying to influence is not just language but how children make sense of their language; and it makes the case that we should not be "intervening" but instead "supporting" the efforts of children to learn how to communicate in everyday life events.

In honor of our being about to experience a turn in a century, and because the situated pragmatics approach calls for historical situatedness, we begin with a look at pragmatics in its historical context (see Chapter 1). We describe a rich set of ideas about pragmatics forwarded by scholars writing in the first half of this century. Chapter 1 samples eight of these scholars and highlights some of their ideas that have pertinence today. In particular, ideas are selected that point to the need for a situated pragmatics, as opposed to an abstract pragmatics. The chapter asks why we have failed to build on these ideas and instead treated pragmatics as revolutionary rather than evolutionary. The chapter answers its own question by arguing that the current approaches to language assessment and intervention are a reaction to behavioral and linguistic approaches to communication.

In Chapter 2 we focus on six domains or contexts: the social context, the emotional context, the functional context, the physical context, the event context, and the discourse context. The contexts provide a framework or context of their own for organizing our thinking about language intervention. These are the contexts which are thematic for much of the rest of the book — they are used to think about the sorts of support children with communicative disorders may need to develop their social and communicative understandings and to make sense of what is going on around them.

Chapter 3 provides an elaboration of three of the six contexts: the social, emotional, and functional contexts. A framework is elaborated for each. Within social context there is a consideration of significance of social roles, their diversity, and the children's degree of affiliation with roles, role recriprocity, and peer relationships. The emotional context is discussed in terms of emotional attunement, social referencing, and maintaining face in social interactions. The importance of communicative goals or intents for communication is emphasized under the rubric of the functional context. Single-act intents are discussed in relation to intents expressed as part of agendas. Ascribing intents to others is also presented as a crucial aspect of communication and worthy of attention as we design our contexts of support.

The physical, event, and discourse contexts are treated in Chapter 4. The physical context is made up of meaningful objects. The arrangement of these objects in physical space provide an invaluable means for supporting children's learning. An argument is made here that children's understandings, even at their most basic levels, need to include more than what is presented in the physical contexts and require a deeper understanding of what objects and pictures mean in relation to each other and to experience. The event context and the discourse context offer a rich set of relationships within which language is understood and communication takes place. These two contexts are detailed in terms of event and discourse types and how they provide those who experience them with a coherent understanding of what is going on.

In Chapter 5 we cycle through the six contextual domains once again, this time to show their role in helping children make sense of their world. The chapter ends with a section on framing, which has to do with how stance, or general interpretive frameworks, needs to be included in our planning of support contexts for children's learning and with a section on how sensemaking concerns can help us choose what to work on and to organize our language intervention approaches.

Culture as a context is treated in Chapter 6. The model's six contexts are discussed here in light of culture. The anthropological literature on the ethnography of communication is presented to fit the six contexts, and consideration is given to how the contexts differ for different cultures. The case is made that everyday life situations are different for children from different cultural backgrounds and that these differences will require different sorts of support within each of the six domains.

Chapter 7 grounds the situated pragmatics approach in the everyday context of school. The six support contexts are discussed in light of children's classroom and playground experiences. Approaches to transitioning children from segregated to included classrooms offer a rich set of possibilities for those working within situated pragmatics, because the effort of the approach is to provide the support children need to be viable and respected members of a social community.

The book ends with two chapters on how situated pragmatics fits with other intervention approaches. In Chapter 8 it is contrasted with behavioral, linguistic, cognitive, information processing, and abstract pragmatics approaches, and treated as parallel to whole language approaches to teaching. In Chapter 9 an argument is made for why situated pragmatic approaches offer a viable alternative for use with children whose learning needs may be linguistic (vocabulary or language structure), and why it is inappropriate to base intervention approaches on a child's diagnosis or presumed developmental level.

I thank:

Nicki Nelson for asking me to write this book;

Rae Sonnenmeier for helping me view what we do as support rather than as intervention;

The embattled professional community dealing with issues of facilitated communication for allowing me the to see that what we do has to do with life, not just language learning;

And facilitated communicators for helping me understand the depth and breadth of support needed to be able to communicate in meaningful ways in everyday life.

Judith Felson Duchan, Ph.D.
State University of New York at Buffalo

To Alan Duchan and Elaine Vanzant
for filling my every day
with optimism and humor.

Prologue

I magine a conversation between John Dewey and his friend William James as they look at current practices in language intervention from their 100-year-old perspective:

James: Well, John how have your ideas fared over the years? Has anyone been paying attention to them?

Dewey: I don't know what to make of it, William. I overhear people paying homage to pragmatics, but they seem to mean something different by it than you and I did. I was concerned much more with morality and how to present ideas to children that could allow them to grow into inquiring adults. These guys seem to be focused on a fixed set of knowledges. Have you noticed how much attention they are paying to teaching children language structure, often to the exclusion of helping children understand what the words and sentences mean in everyday life?

James: Yes, John, there is that problem. But maybe we should be happy to see that there are still those who are working to change educational practices from didactic, rote learning approaches based on a fixed subject matter. Remember when you were fighting that battle to change traditional approaches to progressive ones? I well recall you talking about the importance of experience and "learning by doing." What a shame that the same battles are still being fought nearly a century later. I guess we should be glad that there are still a few people around to work toward your ideals of individualizing goals for learners and structuring the learning enviroment so that children can learn through active experience.

Dewey: What about your ideas, William? Do you see any evidence that they have made an impact on this generation of educators? I remember the "talks to teachers" you gave in 1892. You were focused then on having teachers emphasize the practical side of thought rather than helping children learn abstract ideas.

James: Yes. I took pragmatics to mean the opposite of true reason. I was distinguishing it from those abstract ideas that were being emphasized by other psychologists and philosophers as fundamental to thinking. Remember us talking about what was wrong with Plato and Descarte's idealized forms? Well, I think there is a healthy skepticism about abstract forms in the 1990's version of pragmatics. Teachers and clinicians are not as focused on teaching isolated concepts, and many are focused on helping children experience their everyday worlds in practical ways. But look over there in that school. There is a teacher teaching unrelated words to a child with a language disorder. And look at that clinic. The clinician and child are using picture cards to develop sequencing abilities. Both of those teachers are assuming that knowing words and ordering pictures are skills separable from real-life activities. They would be better off teaching children words that are needed to carry out actions and considering the possibility that the same word heard at different times will take on different associative meanings and that a sequencing can be multiply interpreted depending on one's focus in his or her stream of consciousness.

Dewey: I would have liked to have seen more emphasis by the clinicians and teachers on group projects. My focus on a manual training program during which children learned to understand the world by interacting physically with it is only partially appreciated nowadays. It's what I used to call manual training.

James: Ahhh well, John. Let's go talk to others in our pragmatics club about the good old days and think about how else things might have gone.

Ideas That
Never Took Root

I t was all there in the early part of the twentieth century — all the
ingredients for what we are now proposing as innovative pragmatics intervention. In his *Principles of Psychology,* first published in 1890,
William James made the case that thinking involved making sense of
what was going on as it was happening. In this century's first decade John
Dewey was arguing for practical learning contexts which made everyday sense to the children. In the late 1920s George Herbert Mead was
showing the importance of role taking in children's developing understanding of themselves and others. Malinowski had by 1920 developed
ethnographic methods for carrying out anthropological field work and
had used his methods to elaborate his view that cultural institutions are
created to meet the needs of individual members. By 1927 Grace de
Laguna in her book on children's language learning had shown the importance of social context and pointed out the significance of different
ways language functions for children in the earliest stages of communication. In Russia, Vygotsky was proposing in the 1930s that the way children learn language is by participating in social interactions going on
around them. Bartlett, in 1932, offered several constructs which we
would now take as modern theorizing: the notion of conceptual schemas
which people use in their recall of stories and descriptions; notions of
discourse genres; ideas about how culture influences memory and ima-
gery; and notions about aspects of situational meaning. And Bakhtin by

mid-century had introduced ideas about dialogicality in spoken language and the important role played by speech genre in construction of word and utterance meanings.

This chapter will plumb the ideas of these early twentieth century scholars, selecting from their writings ideas that have applicability from today's view of pragmatics. Contemporary treatments of pragmatics cast it as something new in late twentieth century thinking. Pragmatics notions are treated as revolutionary rather than evolutionary (Duchan, 1984; McTear & Conti-Ramsden, 1992), and as originating in the 1960s rather than the 1900s. Why, if pragmatics ideas were already developed by mid-century, are we not giving homage to our ancestors? There are two intervening theories which broke with the pragmatic tradition being developed in the first part of the twentieth century — behaviorism and structural linguistics. The two traditions were what current pragmatic thinking took as its point of departure. Contemporary theorists of pragmatics have focused on the mistakes of their immediate parents rather than the wisdom of their grandparents. This chapter will present that story by describing the pragmatics notions developed by our distant ancestors, and then the blocks to their evolution focused on by today's innovators in the area of pragmatics.

◼️ SCHOLARS OF PRAGMATICS IN THE EARLY TWENTIETH CENTURY

Current discussions of pragmatics typically locate its origins in the late 1960s with the work in speech-act theory in philosophy (see historical treatments in Duchan, 1984; Lund & Duchan, 1993). Now that we are approaching the turn of another century, it is fitting that we take a centenary perspective on the historical development of pragmatics in the United States. The broader perspective reveals pragmatics ideas dating back to the beginning of the twentieth century. We will single out eight scholars, in particular, and present ideas they developed which we can now incorporate into our current thinking about pragmatics. We will begin with three: William James, John Dewey, and George Herbert Mead. All three scholars knew one another and commented on each other's ideas. All three were linked in the philosophy literature with what was called the "pragmatics movement" — a set of ideas that was in the forefront of scholarly activity in philosophy, psychology, sociology, and education during the first 40 years of this century (Morris, 1970).

The ideas tied to pragmatics were different then. The pragmatics movement for these three scholars took shape in the context of ideas afloat in Europe and America at the beginning of the twentieth century. It was their intent to counter notions, forwarded by Emannuel Kant, that words carried meanings, apart from the contexts in which they occurred. The pragmatists also aimed to separate themselves from the logical positivists such as Bertrand Russell (1905) and A. J. Ayer (1934/1964), who argued that the truth of propositions could be determined through logical examination without looking at how those propositions functioned in the everyday world. Finally, just as for contemporary pragmaticists, there was an effort on the part of our early twentieth century forebearers to counter the developing ideas of behaviorists. Then the concern was to show the errors of behaviorism as developed by John Watson (1914).

The term pragmatics, from the German *pragmatisch*, had to do with rational purpose, and was adopted from Peirce who used it to convey the twofold nature making up rational thought: rational cognition and rational purpose (Peirce, 1931/1958, Vol. 5, p. 412). Pragmatics was favored by Peirce over the term pragmaticism, because the meaning associated with pragmatics involves not just practicalities, practice, or usefulness, but also how knowledge (rational cognition) is related to human action or conduct (rational purpose).

Although the pragmatics movement in American philosophical circles was associated with particular themes, individual scholars had idiosyncratic renditions of what they took to be important about pragmatics. William James sought to create a middle ground between the "tender minded" philosopher with a rationalistic, religious bent and the "tough minded" scientist with an empiricist, fatalistic orientation (James, 1907, cited in White, 1955, p. 136). For Dewey, pragmatics was tied to finding a way to ground philosophy in democratic politics and to better achieve enlightenment through education (Morris, 1970; Rorty, 1979). And George Herbert Mead took as his goal the formulation of an account of social behavior which was more social and complex than the radical behaviorism being heralded at that time by his former student John B. Watson (Mead, 1934).

What makes these thinkers important from today's end-of-the-century perspective is not what they were arguing against or aiming for at the time, but how their ideas enrich our current notions of pragmatics. The following description of their ideas is thereby selective and concentrated on the ideas which fit with present-day frameworks.

William James (1842-1910)

In William James' (1962) psychological view, human beings experience the world as a **stream of consciousness**:

Consciousness . . . does not appear to itself chopped up in bits. Such words as "chain" or "train" do not describe it as fitly as it presents itself in the first instance. It is nothing jointed: it flows. A "river" or "stream" are the metaphors by which it is most naturally described. In talking of it hereafter, lets us call it the stream of thought, of consciousness, or of subjective life. (p. 173)

James conceived the consciousness stream as being divisible into **perchings** and **flights**. The perchings, what he called "substantive parts," are the conclusions; and the flights, the "transitive parts," are the relations and cognitive processes which go on between conclusions (James, 1962, p. 174). In addition, consciousness includes selective **attention** during which thinkers select and create views on what they perceive:

Accentuation and emphasis are present in every perception we have. We find it quite impossible to disperse our attention impartially over a number of impressions. A monotonous succession of sonorous strokes is broken up into rhythms, now of one sort, now of another, by the different accent which we place on different strokes . . . The ubiquity of the distinctions, this and that, here and there, now and then, in our minds is the result of our laying the same selective emphasis on parts of place and time. (p. 184).

How James Related Stream of
Consciousness to Personal Experiences

When Paul and Peter wake up in the same bed, and recognize that they have been asleep, each one of them mentally reaches back and makes connections with but one of the two streams of thought which were broken by the sleeping hours . . . Peter's present instantly finds out Peter's past, and never by mistake knits itself on to that of Paul. Paul's thought in turn is as little liable to go astray. The past thought of Peter is appropriated by the present Peter alone. He may have a knowledge, and a correct one too, of what Paul's last drowsy states of mind were as he sank into sleep, but it is an entirely different sort of knowledge from that which he has of his own last states. He remembers his own states, whilst he only conceives Paul's.

(James, 1962, p. 172–173)

John Dewey (1859–1952)

While James' focus was on how children conceived of the world they live in, John Dewey, his friend and sometime collaborator, worked on developing a curriculum based on those everyday experiences. Dewey was a philosopher who is best known for his founding role in establishing progressive education in America (Cremin, 1959). As part of his educational philosophy he advocated having children experience activities common to their lived-in context (Dewey, 1938, p. 25; 1976, pp. 325–334). When describing the experience-based curriculum of his laboratory school at the University of Chicago, his emphasis was on the relevance the experiences had to the children's lives rather than on their learning of subject matter. He saw knowledge as parallel to tools — not only must a learner gain knowledge, but he or she must also learn how and when to apply the knowledge.

Dewey's educational approach included what was then called **manual training**. The children engaged in physical activities such as cooking and woodworking, during which they talked about what they were doing. In this way they developed insights about the world, such as notions of causality, which could later be extracted from the specific contexts.

Dewey's Description of His Laboratory School's Curriculum

The elementary begins at the age of four and extends to that of thirteen, nine school years. The aims of this period are: (1) to bring the child to an active, inquiring interest in and consciousness of the world of society and nature about him; (2) to bring him to a positive consciousness of his own capacities; and (3) to introduce him gradually to a command of the technical tools required in further work, viz., reading, writing, and number.

The distinguishing aim of this period is not, therefore, to give the child technical facilities, or possession of a certain amount of information. It is to build up in his consciousness an orderly sense of the world in which he lives, working out from that which has most intimately touched him before coming to school, viz., the family and neighborhood life, and gradually extending the range. Orderly

(continued)

> experience of a rich, varied, but consecutive sort, is the aim
> which controls the selection of materials and occupations.
>   (Dewey, 1976, p. 331)

Dewey (1938) did not consider all experiences as educationally productive. Some, he argued, may lead to rote learning and narrow the potential for future learning (p. 26). Others may promote a "slack and careless attitude," which can later prevent the child from approaching future experiences intelligently (p. 26). Or experiences may be disconnected from one another and lead to a dissipation of energy in which the learner "becomes scatter-brained" (p. 26).

Good experiences, according to Dewey, have a high degree of "**agreeableness**" and a high degree of **continuity** with later experiences (Dewey, 1938, p. 27). Thus it is the responsibility of the educator to provide children with experiences that arouse curiosity, strengthen initiative, and build on one another. Dewey further challenges teachers to provide children with experiences that "set up desires and purposes that are sufficiently intense to carry a person over dead places in the future." (Dewey, 1938, p. 38).

Dewey emphasized the importance of purpose in children's construal of educational experiences. For progressive education to be successful, learners need to participate in and identify with the purposes of activities (Dewey, 1938, p. 67). Dewey separated the notion of purpose from those of "impulse" and "desire." "A purpose is an end-view. That is, it involves foresight of the consequences which will result from acting upon impulse" (p. 67). The achievement of purpose often requires planning and understanding the significance of the elements of the experience (p. 68). "It involves (1) observation of surrounding conditions; (2) knowledge of what has happened in similar situations in the past . . . and (3) judgment which puts together what is observed and what is recalled to see what they signify" (p. 69).

Dewey's goal was to create a **child-centered** alternative to the rigidly organized school curricula prevalent at the turn of the twentieth century. He described the earlier, subject-matter approach as one in which the makers of the curricula incorrectly placed too much emphasis on "the logical subdivisions and consecutions of the subject-matter . . . Subject-matter furnishes the end, and it determines method" (Dewey, 1903, p. 8). Dewey countered this doctrinaire, fixed subject-matter approach to education with one in which "Learning is active. It involves reaching out of the mind. It involves organic assimilation starting from within. Literally, we must take our stand with the child and our departure from him.

It is he and not the subject-matter which determines both quality and quantity of learning" (Dewey, 1903, p. 9).

Integral to Dewey's educational approach was his concept of children's **growth**. He focused, in particular, on children's progression from learning through personal experiences to their learning the logic (facts and laws) of particular subject matter. He described this growth as "movement from a social and human center toward a more objective intellectual scheme of organization" (Dewey, 1938, p. 83). Dewey illustrated this growth with examples from children's understanding of causality, in which they proceed from a set of understandings which are first learned from everyday life activities to generalized understandings of causality such as the causal relations involved in scientific research:

> The final justification of shops, kitchens, and so on in the school is not just that they afford opportunity for activity, but that they provide opportunity for the kind of activity or for the acquisition of mechanical skills which leads students to attend to the relation of means and ends, and then to consideration of the way things interact with one another to produce definite effects. It is the same in principle as the ground for laboratories in scientific research. (p. 85)

Dewey was not without his detractors. Benjamin (1939) levied an argument against Dewey's practical approach in a popular book called *Sabre-Tooth Curriculum* (see excerpt below).

**The First Curriculum as Imagined by
Dr. Peddiwell, a Mythical Professor of Education
at a Mythical College Called Petaluma State**

The first great educational theorist and practitioner of whom my imagination has any record was a man of Chellean times whose full name was New-Fist-Hammer-Maker but whom, for convenience, I shall hereafter call New-Fist . . . New-Fist proceeded to construct a curriculum . . . "What things must we tribesmen know how to do in order to live with full bellies, warm backs, and minds free from fear?" he asked himself.

To answer this question, he ran various activities over in his mind. "We have to catch fish with our bare hands in the pool far up the creek beyond that big bend," he said to

(continued)

---

himself. "We have to catch fish with our bare hands in the pool right at the bend. We have to catch them in the same way in the pool just this side of the bend . . ."

Thus New-Fist discovered the first subject of the first curriculum — fish-grabbing-with-the-bare hands.

"Also we club the little woolly horses," he continued with his analysis. "We club them along the bank of the creek where they come down to drink. We club them in the thickets where they lie down to sleep. We club them in the upland meadow where they graze. Wherever we find them we club them."

So woolly-horse-clubbing was seen to be the second main subject in the curriculum.

"And finally, we drive away the saber-tooth tigers with fire," New-Fist went on in his thinking. "We drive them from the mouth of our caves with fire. We drive them from our trail with burning branches. We wave firebrands to drive them from our drinking hole. Always we have to drive them away, and always we drive them with fire."

Thus was discovered the third subject — saber-tooth-tiger-scaring-with-fire.

(Benjamin, 1939, pp. 24–29)

George Herbert Mead (1863–1931)

George Herbert Mead was a philosopher whose work provided the origins for the theory in sociology of symbolic interactionism, in which children's notions of themselves emerge from how they are regarded by others. The sense of another's regard begins with social interactions, whereby the actors when initiating and responding to one another during social exchanges assume the attitude of the other (see the next example).

An Example of the Social Interaction Context of Language Learning

Dogs approaching each other in hostile attitude carry on . . . a language of gestures. They walk around each other,

> growling and snapping, and waiting for the opportunity to attack. Here is a process out of which language might arise, that is, a certain attitude of one individual that calls out a response in the other which in turn calls out a different approach and a different response, and so on indefinitely. In fact, as we shall see, language does arise in just such a process as that.
>
> (Mead, 1934, p. 14)

Central to Mead's conceptualization of interaction is his notion of **perspective**. He argued that individuals, by virtue of their current perceptual viewpoints along with their peculiar experiential history, saw the world differently from one another (Mead, 1932, 1934). Mead (1934) provides us with an example to illustrate his point:

> Different positions will lead to different experiences in regard to such an object as a penny placed on a certain spot . . . What the penny would be experienced as depends upon the past experiences that may have occurred to the different individuals. It is a different penny to one person from what it is to another; yet the penny is there as an entity by itself (p. 31).

Mead (1934) extended his notion of idiosyncratic perceptual and historical perspective to children's language learning as well as their learning about their own and others' roles in social interaction. He viewed early language learning as social, as exemplified in his description of how a vocal gesture is seen from one's own as well as the other person's point of view.

> We are unconsciously putting ourselves in the place of others and acting as others act . . . We are, especially through the use of the vocal gestures, continually arousing in ourselves those responses which we call out in other persons, so that we are taking the attitudes of the other persons into our own conduct. The critical importance of language in the development of human experience lies in this fact that the stimulus is one that can react upon the speaking individual as it reacts upon the other. (p. 69)

Of central concern to Mead (1934) was how humans come to think about themselves. He referred to this as an individual's **self-consciousness** and saw it developing from an individual's sense of how he or she is regarded by others:

The individual experiences himself as such, not directly, but only indirectly, from particular standpoints of other individual members of the same social group, or from the generalized standpoint of the social group as a whole to which he belongs. For he enters his own experience as a self or individual, not directly or immediately, not by becoming a subject to himself, but only in so far as he first becomes an object to himself just as other individuals are objects to him or in his experience and he becomes an object to himself only by taking the attitudes of other individuals toward himself within a social environment or context of experience and the behavior in which both he and they are involved. (p. 138)

Mead's social interaction theory took into account the variety of roles required in different life events. He discussed these roles in relation to play events occurring early in life and to games occurring later. In play the child assumes the roles of the various characters in the scenario, one at a time, and thereby attains the notion of different perspectives on what is taking place. In games the child assumes the roles of all the participants at once, as part of the understanding of the rules of the event. In both play and games the child's sense of self is determined by his sense of the others' roles — in play the role of a specific other and in games a generalized other.

The three progenitors of pragmatics developed ideas that were not taken up by later generations of scholars. The pragmatics movement was soon to dissipate as a movement in America. The pragmatists of this period were not alone in their interest in contextual factors related to language and communication. Others from the fields of anthropology, psychology, and literary theory contributed concepts which are being reevaluated in light of contemporary thinking about pragmatics.

Bronislaw Malinowski (1884–1942)

Some say that Bronislaw Malinowski originated modern-day anthropology. He developed what has come to be called the **functionalist approach** to understanding culture. The approach assumed that cultural customs arose from the needs of the individual members of the culture, and that different customs were functionally related.

Best known for his study of the people living on the Trobriand Islands off New Guinea, Malinowski was among the first anthropologists to live with those he studied and to take as his enterprise the discovery of his subjects' cultural understandings. He was among the first of the anthropologists to forward a view of **cultural relativity** which is commonly accepted in today's approaches to achieving multicultural sensitivity. At the turn of the century, Malinowski was unusual in holding the belief that members of different cultures have different world views arising from different self-understandings, social interactions, language use, and cultural customs (Clifford, 1988).

Malinowski is also known for his innovations in ethnographic methods which included charting activities to determine the range of customs, taking field notes of observations about how social customs are carried out, and collecting statements and narratives from the people engaging in the customs "as documents of native mentality" (Kuper, 1983, pp. 15–16). He was perhaps the first to carry out research as a **participant observer**.

Malinowski's Approach to Studying Cultural Events, Which He Called "the Imponderabilia of Everyday Life"

In working out the rules and regularities of native custom, and in obtaining a precise formula for them from the collection of data and native statements, we find that this very precision is foreign to real life, which never adheres rigidly to any rules. It must be supplemented by the observation of the manner in which a given custom is carried out, of the behavior of the natives in obeying the rules so exactly formulated by the ethnographer, of the very exceptions which in sociological phenomena almost always occur.

(Kuper, 1983, pp. 15–16)

Grace de Laguna (1878–1978)

Grace Andrus de Laguna, in a book written in 1927 and reissued in 1963, put forward her theory of how language evolves to serve social control functions, in both the evolution of the human species as well as the development of young children. She contended that nonhuman animals' communications serve two general functions: to signal others to pay attention to them, as in the cry of courtship, and to signal others to attend to something in the environment, as in cries that warn of danger. Humans, on the other hand, learn to use language to express a greater variety of communicative functions, such as ones which serve to proclaim, command, and question.

Proclamations, according to de Laguna, are speech acts that function as an indicator of things as well as announcement of what it is that is interesting about them (de Laguna, 1963, p. 75). She divided proclamations into four general types: (1) ones that specify the presence or existence of something; (2) ones that indicate something important about that thing (the predicative function); (3) ones that announce an intended act; and (4) ones that announce or describe an act already completed.

The issuance of proclamations, as well as commands and questions, is carried out in the context of the children's notions about the "personal order" of the world around them. The order is a social-emotional one, involving feelings of well-being. De Laguna illustrates functions of speech as follows:

How Speech Functions Within a Social Order

Men do not speak simply to relieve their feelings or to air their views, but to awaken a response in their fellows and to influence their attitudes and acts. It is further the means by which men are brought into a new and momentous relationship with the external world, the very relationship which makes the world for them an objective order.

(de Laguna, 1963, pp. 19–20)

The order of the world as seen in the perspective of the attitudes and possible acts of others — a world characterized by favor and disfavor, help and hindrance, benefit and injury, intention and purpose, good and evil and the whole system of properties of living beings in their relations to each other.

(de Laguna, 1963, p. 215)

Lev Vygotsky (1896–1934)

Lev Vygotsky was in Russia at the turn of the century, developing a social-historical theory of learning which was destined to create a stir among scholars and educators in America some 50 years later, well after his death (e.g., see Tharp & Gallimore, 1988; Wertsch, 1985a, 1985b, 1991).

Vygotsky contributed a number of ideas to current theorizing in pragmatics. One was his notion that knowledge, including language knowledge, is learned first as **socio-cultural knowledge** and is later internalized as inner speech. A second idea inherited from Vygotsky was that intelligence consists not only of what is known but of how well one can extend that knowledge when provided with appropriate assistance (i.e., assistance within their intellectual grasp). Vygotsky described an area or zone between what children know and what they can learn with assistance. He called the zone between what is originally known and what is learned with assistance (and retained later with no assistance) the **zone of proximal development** (Vygotsky, 1978). Vygotsky saw development as involving meaningful understandings rather than merely skill learning. The recent followers of Vygotsky outline three steps for teachers to pay attention to as they offer assistance with the child's zone: (1) determining the child's level of performance; (2) providing assisted performance; and (3) evaluating the child's new learning in a context of independence (Moll, 1992, p. 7).

Vygotsky's Notion of the Zone of Proximal Development

Suppose I investigate two children upon entrance into school, both of whom are ten years old chronologically and eight years old in terms of mental development. Can I say that they are the same age mentally? Of course. What does this mean? It means that they can independently deal with tasks up to the degree of difficulty that has been standardized for the eight year old level. If I stop at this point, people would imagine that the subsequent course of mental development and of school learning for these children will be the same, because it depends on their intellect . . . Now imagine that I do not terminate my study at this point, but only begin it. These children seem to be capable of handling problems up to an eight-year-old's level, but not beyond that. Suppose that I show them various ways of dealing with the problem. Different experimenters might employ different modes of demonstration in different cases: some might run through an entire demonstration and ask the children to repeat it, others might initiate the solution and ask the child to finish it, or offer leading questions. In short, in some way or another I propose that the children solve the problem with my assistance. Under these circumstances it turns out that the first child can deal with problems up to a twelve-year-old's level, the second up to a nine-year-old's. Now are these children mentally the same?

When it was first shown that the capability of children with equal levels of mental development to learn under a

(continued)

> teacher's guidance varied to a high degree, it became apparent that those children were not mentally the same age and that the subsequent course of their learning would obviously be different. This difference between twelve and eight, or between nine and eight, is what we call the zone of proximal development. It is the distance between the actual developmental level as determined by independent problem solving and the level of potential development as determined through problem solving under adult guidance or in collaboration with more capable peers.
>
> (Vygotsky, 1978, pp. 85–86.)

Frederick Charles Bartlett (1886–1969)

Frederick Bartlett was a British psychologist who published an influential book on "remembering" in the year 1932 in which he introduced the notion of schema as a structure of memory. Bartlett reported in his book the results of a group of studies in which he asked adults to read stories and describe scenes. He then asked his subjects to recall what they read or saw several times over a protracted period (up to 6½ years). Bartlett also had his subjects engage in a version of the parlor game "gossip" in which he told a story to one person and had that person tell another, and so on, in a procedure which he called "the method of serial reproduction" (Bartlett, 1932, pp. 118–119). For both recall and serial reproduction procedures Bartlett compared the recollections of the same person over time, of different people with each other over time, and of all recollections with the original story. He discovered regularities across and within subjects as exemplified by his rendition of how his subjects handled unusual elements in a story of an Indian who had "something black" come out of his mouth.

> ### Changes in the Recollections of Subjects
> ### Under the Method of Serial Reproduction
>
> In the original version of a story which Bartlett had subjects read and then recall, he described the death of an Indian as follows:

> When the sun rose he fell down. Something black came out of his mouth. His face became contorted.
>
> Bartlett's reported how the recalled versions of different subjects changed over a period of time. Some examples are:
>
> When the sun rose he fell down. And he gave a cry, and as he opened his mouth a black thing rushed from it.
>
> When the sun rose he suddenly felt faint, and when he would have risen he fell down, and a black thing rushed out of his mouth.
>
> He felt no pain until sunrise the next day, when, on trying to rise, a great black thing flew out of his mouth.
>
> He lived that night, and the next day, but at sunset his soul fled black from his mouth.
>
> He lived during the night and the next day, but died at sunset, and his soul passed out from his mouth.
>
> Bartlett commented about the "rationalizations" of his subjects which created the distortions in recollection:
>
> First the "something black" gains a kind of force or vivacity of its own: "it rushed out"; then, "it flew out". Then the activity receives explanation, for the black thing becomes the man's soul, and, by a common conventional phrase, it is said to have "passed out". Once the soul is introduced, the mysterious blackness can be dropped, and this speedily occurs.
>
> (Bartlett, 1932, p. 127)

In his treatment of meaning, Bartlett alludes to the process of what some (but not Bartlett, himself) have called "sensemaking" (Bartlett, 1932, Chapter 12). He observed from the recall patterns of his subjects that they focused on particular aspects of the narrative or description, and that this focus remained in their later renditions of the story. The focused elements tended to be things that struck the fancy of an individual, were salient in the culture, or dominant in the situation. From these elements the subjects constructed coherence out of their perceived or recalled experiences — a coherence Bartlett described as a structured schema.

Mikhail Bakhtin (1895–1975)

Bakhtin was a Russian philosopher and literary analyst whose work spanned from the 1920s until his death in 1975. His ideas have received wide attention from scholars in fields as disparate as literary criticism (Todorov, 1984), classics in the study of ancient texts (Felson-Rubin, 1992), and child development (Wertsch, 1991).

A central focus of Bakhtin's early work was his discovery of how spoken as well as written utterances contain a variety of perspectives, what Bakhtin (1981) called **multiple voices**. For example, an utterance that contains a direct quote can be thought of as being expressed in the voice of the person doing the quoting as well as the person being quoted. Or an utterance in which a person is mocking another is said in two voices, that of the mocker and the target of the mockery.

In an elaboration of the notion of multivocality, Bakhtin (1981) also proposed that a speaker or writer addresses all verbal expressions to an audience and in so doing creates a perspective for the expression which is dialogical. If, for example, an utterance is an answer to a prior question, it carries in it the history of that question and in this way has a dialogical focus.

Although verbal expressions all are seen by Bakhtin as having multiple voices, the voices differ in strength for different utterances. Some expressions, such as those said by teachers or which appear in expository writing of textbooks, have an **authoritarian voice** and leave little room for open dialog or multiple interpretation. Other utterances, such as those of emotions said in an **expressive voice** (e.g., I want some!), are the strongest expressions of the speaker's or writer's voice, and have less influence from an addressee.

Besides offering insights into how utterances can contain a variety of voices, Bakhtin also demonstrated how the interpretation of utterances is governed by the **speech genre** or speech event in which they occur (Bakhtin, 1986). Bakhtin's notion of speech genre included oral narratives, commentary, scientific statements, proverbs, novels, and "short rejoinders of daily dialogue" (Bakhtin 1986, pp. 60–61).

Bakhtin indicates his sensitivity to voice, in the example in the box below, where he shows how a mundane sentence that describes an everyday event is unlikely to occur in contexts where the speaker expresses the obvious. Rather, such a statement, when offered in a situated context, is likely to be an observation that the current state of green grass is different than what we have been experiencing — say, a brown grass period characteristic of winter.

**Bakhtin on How Meaning Is Tied
to the Situational and Social Context**

The speaker sees that the grass is green and announces:
"The grass is green." Such senseless "communications"
are often directly regarded as classic examples of the sentence. But in reality any communication like that, addressed to someone or evoking something, has a particular purpose, that is, it is a real link in the chain of speech
communication in a particular sphere of human activity or
everyday life.

(Bakhtin, 1986, p. 83)

Summary of Early Pragmatics

A number of scholars with pragmatic predilections made contributions
during the first half of the twentieth century. As a group they offer us
important insights, some yet to be rediscovered, about how language fits
with other things going on in the experience of those using it. As can be
seen by the variety of ideas summarized in the list in Table 1–1, the rich-
ness of their ideas, had they remained in the foreground, would have
created a very different approach to language intervention developed in
the second half of the twentieth century.

■❏ BLOCKS TO THE ADVANCEMENT OF PRAGMATICS THEORY AND PRACTICE

What happened to these old ideas that have such contemporary relevance? Why weren't they carried into the mid-century by scholars or
clinicians who created intervention approaches in the area of communication disorders? In this section we will describe the theories that re-
placed the pragmatically focused orientations. The replacements were
from frameworks incompatible with earlier pragmatic theories in that
they were designed to control or ignore context rather than explore its
effects on communication. The context-sensitive frameworks were re-
placed with frameworks brought in by behaviorists and structural lin-
guists whose ideas became mainstream approaches in America in the
latter half of the twentieth century.

TABLE 1-1

Summary of Ideas from the First Half of the Twentieth Century That Have Relevance for Today's Pragmatic Interventions.

1. Reality is experienced as a seamless flow, a stream of consciousness, within which one can select elements for attention and organize them into units of awareness — conceptual "perchings." (James)

2. Experiences differ in educational value, depending on student interest and how they relate to what the student already knows. Education should be child-centered. (James & Dewey)

3. Knowledge should be treated as a tool to be used in situated contexts. (Dewey)

4. Active, hands-on experience, such as that indicative of manual training, enhances learning. (Dewey)

5. Educational experiences should be designed to build on one another, creating a continuum of learning and facilitating intellectual growth. (Dewey)

6. Educational experiences should involve purposive goal-seeking accompanied by reflection. (Dewey)

7. Language is based in social interaction wherein partners respond to one another and take one another's perspective. (Mead)

8. Self-consciousness develops from experiencing the attitudes of others in social events. (Mead)

9. Cultural customs serve important psychological and social functions for the members of the culture. (Malinowski)

10. Culture promotes different world views. (Malinowski)

11. Language can serve a variety of communicative functions. (de Laguna)

12. Language is carried out in the context of a personal-social-emotional order. (de Laguna)

13. Language learning is based on socio-cultural experiences. (Vygotsky)

14. Learning occurs when assistance is provided within the child's zone of potential learning or, in Vygotsky's phraseology, zone of proximal development. (Vygotsky)

15. Memory is influenced by situational experiences and cultural interests, and is structured in coherent conceptual schemas. (Bartlett)

16. Utterances are influenced by the surrounding discourse and are expressions of multiple points of view. (Bakhtin)

17. The speech genre or ongoing event governs the interpretation of utterances. (Bakhtin)

American Behaviorism, Its Origins

J. B. Watson (1878–1958) and B. F. Skinner (1904–1990) were working out the details of behavioristic psychology at the beginning of this century, alongside the pragmatic scholars. Indeed, Watson was a student of George Herbert Mead at the University of Chicago. Many of the scholars whose ideas we now can integrate into our pragmatics thinking wrote of their differences with behaviorism. But their counterarguments were not persuasive, and they eventually lost to the behaviorists who had a much greater influence on future generations of scholars and professionals in the areas of language learning and language intervention.

Operant Conditioning Approaches

Operant conditioning, developed by Skinner in 1938, holds that a learned response or change in behavior depends on alterations in the stimulus context preceding the new behavior as well as on the reinforcing context following the new behavior. The stimulus events which occur prior to the response are called **antecedent events** or **discriminative stimuli** or **prompts**. Those occurring after the response has been made are **consequent events** or **reinforcement**. Because the response to be learned is viewed as being controlled by the contingent antecedents and consequents, Skinner's method when applied to intervention is sometimes called **contingency management**. The aim of the method is to modify or manage the child's behavior, thereby earning the name **behavior modification** or **behavior management**.

These notions indigenous to behaviorism presume that learning takes place in small, incremental steps and that what is learned then is added together to form larger wholes. If the task to be learned is a complex one, such as that involved in the imitation of a word, the approach is to divide the word into its components, such as sounds, to teach the sounds first, and then build in sequential steps to the word. Thus the approach is one of **atomism** — building up from the smallest units or atoms to the larger wholes.

Behaviorists from the 1940s to the present subscribe to the empiricist notion that what is to be manipulated and learned are associations. So, a program may be designed to teach children that stimuli in a set are associated with one another, for example, teaching children to associate together stimuli with similar attributes in an attempt to help them learn how objects are constituted and related. Or an intervention program may be designed to teach children to associate a response with a given stimulus or stimuli, such as having them name an object. A program may also be organized to teach children to associate several responses with one another, for example, several words with one another in the construction of a phrase. Finally, a behavioral program may be planned to get children to associate a given response with its consequents, such as having the child learn that a response will be followed by a positive reinforcement, with the aim of increasing the likelihood that the desired response will occur again. This notion of **associationism** is basic to behaviorism, a learning theory which presumes that learning is the process of making new associations whether they are between stimuli, between stimuli and responses, between responses or between responses and reinforcements.

The presumption for which behaviorism is most noted is its **peripheralism**, which allows in its realm of theorizing only events that are observable, countable, and measurable. Constructs other than observable stimuli or responses are seen as within an unknowable "black box," and thereby eliminated from consideration. Thus mental constructs such schemas, concepts, or abstract rules are not allowed. An individual's behaviors become the focus, rather than what that person may be thinking to cause those behaviors. Peripheralism's opposite is mentalism.

An example of a an early language therapy program which was based in behaviorism was that of Lovaas (1968). The program consisted of training 10 nonverbal autistic children to produce words. Lovaas first provided the children with a discriminative stimulus, a speech sound, and then reinforced them for imitating the sound. Once a child learned to respond to the stimulus, Lovaas proceeded to reinforcing imitated syllables and then progressed to words. Once the child was imitating words, he or she was presented with an object to associate with the word (e.g., a ball was shown and the children were reinforced for saying "ball").

A primary aim of behavioral language programs, besides having the child learning a new behavioral response, is to have a newly learned behavioral response spread or **generalize** from the original and particularized stimulus-response-reinforcement constellation in the training conditions to other similar conditions. According to behavioral theory generalization can occur in a variety of ways. A learned behavior may generalize by occurring in response to not only the particular discriminative stimulus used in the training session, but to other similar stimuli — a condition called **stimulus equivalence**. Or a learned response may generalize when behaviors similar but not identical to the one already learned occur in response to the original discriminative stimulus — a circumstance described as **response generalization**.

If a child learns to say "ball" in response to a particular ball, and then learns to say "ball" in response to a second ball which is larger and of a different color, stimulus generalization is said to have occurred. Similarly, if the child says "ball" to the first ball at first, and then later says "little ball" in response to the same ball, response generalization is evidenced. In both cases, the child has exhibited generalization from his or her original learning. Behaviorists devote considerable attention to generalization when they design language learning programs for language-impaired children.

Table 1–2 provides a brief list of the basic concepts found in behavioral theory when applied to language intervention.

TABLE 1–2
Central Notions of Behavioral Theory.

1. **Operant conditioning, contingency management, behavior modification, behavior management:** the various names of the method that aims to change a child's responses by manipulating the conditions surrounding it (stimuli and reinforcements).

2. **Antecedent events, discriminative stimuli, or prompts:** aspects of the conditions presented to the child or selected by the child which control the child's subsequent response.

3. **Consequent events, reinforcement:** aspects of the conditions that occur after the child responds which increase (positive reinforcement) or decrease (negative reinforcement) the likelihood for that response to occur again.

4. **Stimulus equivalence:** when a new stimulus, because of its likeness (physical or abstract) to an old stimulus, triggers the same response as the old stimulus. The new stimulus is said to be equivalent to the original one in that both control the same behavior.

5. **Response generalization:** when a new response is associated with a stimulus, a response that is similar but not identical to the one previously associated with that stimulus.

6. **Atomism:** learning progresses in small, incremental steps. Elements that are the atoms are learned first and then add together to form larger and more complex wholes.

7. **Associationism:** learning is the process of making new associations between stimulus elements, stimuli and responses, or response elements.

8. **Peripheralism:** learning can be observed by examining the relationship between a behavior and its antecedent and consequent conditions. The focus is on what can be observed and measured.

Soft Behaviorism: Incidental and Milieu Teaching

The first language programs to use behavioral techniques appeared in the late 1960s. They were didactic in nature A teacher-trainer presented stimuli for the child to imitate, and then reinforced the child's imitations which approximated the model (Gray & Fygetakis, 1968; Guess, Sailor, Rutherford & Baer, 1968; Lovaas, Berberich, Perloff, & Schaeffer, 1966; Sloane & MacAuley, 1968).

In the mid- and late 1970s a new behavioral method was designed — one that was less didactic and more naturalistic (Hart & Risley, 1968; Hart & Rogers-Warren, 1978). Called **incidental teaching** or a **milieu approach**, the method did not require trainer initiations, but rather placed the trainer in a role that was responsive to the child's initiations. The context for learning was in the child's milieu, and the trainer reinforced desired responses using rewards that fit with what was going on. The focus was on getting the child to communicate his or her needs, not just on producing a targeted response. (For a more detailed historical account of behavioral approaches to language intervention, see Bricker [1993]).

To carry out a program of incidental teaching, the teacher arranged the environment to elicit a targeted response from the child and followed that response by requesting elaboration if needed or providing a reinforcement if the response was adequate. (See Table 1–3 for an example of the types of techniques used to elicit a child's request using a milieu approach.)

Structural Linguistics and Language Intervention

At about the same time that behaviorism was catching on as a model for language learning, structural linguistics became an established model for how language was organized. The earliest approaches for working with language-impaired children presumed that language knowledge is abstract and decontextualized and further that language is made up of sounds and morphemes, which are assembled according to prescribed syntactic rules to form phrases and sentences. The notion was that levels of language training are separable and should be worked with separately when designing intervention programs (see Table 1–4 for examples of linguistic teaching programs designed for different language areas).

These linguistic teaching approaches were based on what Chomsky (1965) called surface structures. They involved teaching children sounds

TABLE 1–3
An Example of Techniques Used During Incidental or Milieu Teaching Aimed at Getting a Child to Initiate a Request.

Technique	Description
Stimulus setting	The teacher or clinician places desirable objects in the child's view but out of the child's reach (stimulus setting).
Time delay	The adult waits for the child to respond.
Focused attention	If the wait is insufficient to elicit a response, the adult asks a question (e.g., "What do you want?").
Confirmation	If the child answers, the adult confirms the answer and models the targeted structure (e.g., "Oh, I see, you want paint"). The adult then gives the child the paint.
Mand model	If the child does not answer, the adult prompts again (e.g., "Bob, say, I want the paint").
Confirmation	If the child responds to the prompt, the adult gives the child the paint and positively reinforces the response verbally (e.g., "Very good. You want the paint. Here it is").

via articulation therapies, words via programs to teach basic vocabulary and associated concepts, and grammar via programs to teach inflectional morphemes, parts of speech, and various phrase and sentence structures. Many of the programs required children to imitate language forms presented to them and followed the behaviorist assumptions that learning occurs from reinforced stimulus-response associations.

Also included in these early linguistic programs were those aimed at teaching children to associate meaning with single morphemes and two-morpheme combinations. These semantic programs assume language understanding begins with single morphemes, the smallest linguistic elements in the language that carry meaningful content. Once children learn to associate meanings with isolated morphemes (lexical or vocabulary training), they are presented with two-morpheme combinations. In this case the focus of the intervention was on teaching children semantic relations. (See Table 1–4 for some early as well as more recent examples.)

TABLE 1-4
Examples of Research on Intervention Programs Targeting Different
Linguistic Structures (1960s through 1970s).

Program	Description	Research Studies
Vocabulary	Programs that present pictured referents and provide the child with an associated word.	Bricker & Bricker, 1974; Gillham, 1979; Guess, Sailor, & Baer, 1974; Kent, 1974; Whitehurst, Novak, & Zorn, 1972
Inflectional morphemes	Programs that provide the child with examples of word endings to imitate and then use productively.	Baer & Guess, 1973; Gray & Fygetakis, 1968; Guess, Sailor, Rutherford, & Baer, 1968
Word classes	Programs designed to teach children particular parts of speech such as auxiliaries, adjectives, or pronouns.	Auxiliaries: Culatta & Horn, 1982; Hegde, 1980. Adjectives: Hart & Risley, 1968. Pronouns: Hegde & Gierut, 1979
Syntax	Programs designed to help children learn various aspects of syntax.	Fokes, 1976; Lee, Koenigsknecht & Mulhern, 1975; Mulac & Tomlinson, 1977; Zweitman & Sonderman, 1979
Semantic relations	Programs that facilitate children's understanding of the meaning relations in two-word utterances.	Jeffree, Wheldall, & Mittler, 1973; Leonard, 1975; MacDonald, Blott, Gordon, Spiegel, & Hartmann, 1974; Miller & Yoder, 1974

In keeping with the structural tradition, recent structural approaches to language teaching have included discourse structures — units of structure that include more than single sentences. For example, new programs are aimed at teaching children the structures dictated from story grammars, wherein a story is seen as consisting of several required units that can be abstracted from any story (Klecan-Aker, 1993).

■ SUMMARY

This chapter began by presenting the ideas of early twentieth century scholars and finding in them the seeds of many of today's pragmatics "discoveries." When placing pragmatics in its proper historical context, one cannot claim, as we have, that our current views are revolutionary (Duchan, 1984; McTear & Conti-Ramsden, 1992). They were thought of nearly a century ago. Nor can the current approaches be considered as evolutionary, because current advances do not seem to be based in those early ideas. Contemporary supporters of pragmatics theories or practice typically do not draw from the rich heritage available from these early twentieth century scholars.

The reason for our failure to appreciate our ancestors is that we are busy trying to understand pragmatics advances in a more recent context — that offered by behaviorism and linguistics. Both of these traditions have led to clinical approaches that separate what is taught from its contextual use, from its understanding as part of a general understanding about what is going on during everyday life communications. This book is aimed at putting context back into learning.

The Reemergence of Pragmatics

oday's notions of pragmatics come in many versions, some restricted, others more encompassing. Most renditions of pragmatics define it in terms of its relationship to language structure. Taking this language-based orientation, researchers and clinicians have depicted pragmatics as what is left of language after removing content and form (Lahey, 1988; Smith & Leinonen, 1992). Others, with more of a linguistic bent, may see pragmatics as an added component of language structure (McTear & Conti-Ramsden, 1992, p. 8).

The version of pragmatics adopted here does not take language structure as its point of departure. Rather, it is what I have called elsewhere the "hot" version (Duchan, 1984, p. 178). In this more radical view of pragmatics, domains previously seen as peripheral are made central to communication. Language structure in this situated pragmatics is but one domain among many that needs to be considered when designing language intervention programs.

Following the lead of this century's early pragmatic theoreticians, we can identify at least six contexts or domains that constitute children's developing communication abilities. Each has implications for helping children communicate better, and all need to be included in the effort to create approaches to language intervention.

■□ SIX CONTEXTS THAT SURROUND, INFLUENCE, AND CONSTITUTE COMMUNICATION

1. The Social Context

George Herbert Mead portrayed language learning and communication as emerging from one's expected role in a social context. Mead's ideas evolved into what is now the theory of **symbolic interactionism**, sometimes referred to as the "looking-glass" theory of the self (Reynolds, 1993). His idea was that individuals define themselves in light of how others regard them. Rather than treat what others think of them as a reflection of themselves, they consider themselves to be reflections of how they are treated. So, a child misdiagnosed as retarded or language impaired is obliged by the way he or she is treated to develop a self-image of incompetence and carry out his or her communications within that assigned role — incompetence.

The looking-glass definition of self depends on the learners' understanding what others think of them. The ideas learners have about the thoughts of their partners need to be in keeping with the role reciprocity between the two. Thus learners enact their roles in relation to the roles they ascribe to others. Roles of student, younger brother, and customer are played out in relation to the reciprocal roles assumed by their interactants (e.g., teacher, older brother, and clerk).

Modern-day symbolic interactionism includes in it notions of **role choices** (Spreitzer, Snyder, & Larson, 1979; Stryker & Statham, 1985) and **role distance** (Goffman, 1961). (For reviews see Reynolds, 1993, and Stryker & Statham, 1985.) Individuals who have many role options available have been shown to be more satisfied with their lives than those who are cast in but a few roles (Stryker & Stratham). Moreover, those with few roles tend to have restricted access to societies' rewards. Further, when playing out a role, individuals may feel directly identified with it or distanced from it. For example, someone who is competent would be less enthusiastic and less identified with a role that underestimates his or her competence.

Another area of social context, which offers the communicator an important view of what is going on, is the way children think about their interactants. The elaborateness of their notions of the other will feed their notions of **role reciprocity**, as well as in some cases provide a better understanding of what is expected of them and of the cultural meaning of the event.

Finally, the communicators' interest in engaging in social interactions and their ability to do so is crucial in achieving success in everyday communications. And the way others, especially their peers, regard them and accept them will affect their future willingness to participate in social interactions, regardless of their abilities. Thus, **peer relationships** are affected by children's willingness to engage in peer interactions and their ability to be part of what is going on, as well as the willingness of others to accept them in their social activities.

The following box lists the aspects of social contexts that can be targeted as domains for consideration when conducting language intervention and providing contextual support for children's learning. The domains are general ones, and what is provided in each would depend on the developmental level of the targeted children and their communicative needs. For example, role understandings and enhancing role diversity in early development may involve supporting and extending a child's role learning in a family during daily life activities. Enhancing role diversity later in a child's life may involve helping the child understand the various role relations and diverse roles inherent in school interactions.

**Types of Support
That Can Be Provided By
a Clinician, Teacher, or Parent to
Aid Children's Social Learnings**

Role relations: Helping children understand their assigned roles.

Role diversity: Working to provide children with different roles when they participate in real as well as imaginary activities.

Role distance: Helping children identify with their assigned roles.

Role reciprocity: Working with children to understand their roles in relation to roles of others in an interaction.

Peer relationships: Working with children and their peers to create facilitatory role relations in their everyday activities.

2. The Emotional Context

In 1927 Grace de Laguna (1963/1927) depicted language as achieving goals which are generated from one's understandings of a social-emotional world order. De Laguna provides a hint of what she means by listing domains of feeling which the language learner attunes to. Among the emotional contexts that make up the personal order are: favor and disfavor, help and hindrance, and benefit and injury (see page 12).

Four separable and detailed explications of emotion now exist in several literatures. Each offers ways for thinking about emotion as part of the communication exchange. The first is **affect attunement**, coming from the research and theorizing of Daniel Stern. Stern identified affect attunement as a way that interactants respond to one anothers' emotional tone. One type of tone identified by Stern is that of body vitality. Vitality affect conveys qualities of feeling such as "surging," "fading away," and "drawn out" (Stern, 1985, p. 54). A second type of emotional tone, and the type most commonly associated with the domain of emotion, is the expression of discrete emotional states such as anger, fear, happiness, shame, or embarrassment.

A second way affect is communicated has been identified as **social referencing** (see Stern, 1985, and Walden, 1993, for reviews). Social referencing occurs in situations of stress or uncertainty and involves the child's reliance on the affective expressions of an accompanying adult to decide how to feel about what is going on (Walden, 1993).

Empowerment, a third area of affect's influence on communication, is usually taken as a way to allow or help others to assume control of their own life decisions with the aim of achieving self-determination (Dunst, Trivette, & Deal, 1988). Dunst et al. have designed procedures to provide families and individuals with disabilities with the skills and power to make their own life decisions. In so doing, individuals are given a chance to develop self-confidence and self-determination.

Finally, another area of affect studied by those doing cross-cultural research has to do with the culture's ways of allowing its members to avoid embarrassment — to save face. In the mainstream of white, middle class America, children with communication disorders are prone to experience failure and ridicule and to be socially ostracized. A possible ramification of such experiences is a predilection to become withdrawn and unresponsive to social initiatives. This "learned helplessness" is a frequent offshoot of lack of communicative success and can be seen as a legitimate attempt on the children's part to "save face." Therefore, intervention designed to create contexts that are free of embarrassment, contexts involving **face saving**, becomes a viable and needed enterprise.

The following list includes four types of emotional support that a language interventionist can provide a child during the course of facilitating his or her growth in communication.

**Types of Affect or Emotional Support
That Can Be Provided to
Aid a Child's Social Learning**

Affect attunement: Creating consistent interactions between a child and family members and friends which involve matching that child's emotional state in body vitality, rhythm, movement, or verbal content.

Social referencing: Providing the child with affective cues about how he or she should feel about new situations.

Empowerment: Creating contexts in which the child can take a valued and important role, leading to positive sense of self-esteem.

Maintaining face: Preventing or altering situations so that a child is not likely to be made to feel embarrassed or inept.

---

3. The Functional Context

In 1927 de Laguna recognized that language served communicative functions such as proclaiming and requesting. These functions were associated with individual utterances. Today we call them "speech acts."

Despite the contributions of de Laguna in 1927, the discovery of speech acts is usually attributed to two language philosophers, Austin (1962) and John Searle (1969), the developers of modern-day speech act theory. These scholars argued that sentences should not be regarded as statements, but rather as functional expressions of intentionality. A speech act had three components, according to Searle, an illocutionary force which was the issuer's intent, a locutionary part which was the sentence used to express the intent, and a perlocutionary effect which related to how the act was responded to. Of the three components, it was the illocutionary force, or intent, which was taken up by those working with children, and interventions were designed to help children create and communicate a variety of intentional acts. The acts, such as requests, comments, greetings, or acknowledgments, were delivered during the course of everyday communications, as single acts in naturally occurring contexts. They will be referred to here as **single act intents** to differentiate them from intents expressed over the course of an event or discourse. Examples of discourse intents are: entertaining an audience throughout a story-telling episode, or persuading an audience during an argument. These discourse or event-based intents have been called **agendas** (Lund & Duchan, 1993).

Agendas, like single act intents can be inferred from an individual's communications and, when put together, show a design aimed at accomplishing a communicative goal. The most obvious example of an agenda is found in persuasive discourse in which one person's aim is to convince another of something. Many sentences in a discourse of persuasion work together to accomplish a single agenda — to persuade an audience.

Communicators not only need support in initiating and expressing their intents and agendas, they also must be able to identify and respond to others' intents and agendas. A third area of intentionality is thus one in which the child is provided with support and information about how to detect the motivations behind the behavior and language of their communicative partners. This area of **ascribing motivations to others** has been studied in the developmental literature under various topics: perspective taking, theory of mind, understanding subjectivity.

The three areas which can be a focus of intervention to provide the child with support for communicating his or her own intents and agendas and in understanding and responding to the intents and agendas conveyed by his or her communication partners, are:

**Areas for Supporting Children's Efforts
to Create and Achieve Intentional Goals
and Respond to the Motivations
Expressed by Others**

Single act intents: Helping the child learn how to associate intent with communicative acts, either nonverbal (e.g., a point designed as a request to get someone to look) or verbal (e.g., using a word, phrase, or sentence to make a request).

Agendas: Modeling or supporting the child's efforts to plan a series of acts to achieve a unified goal (e.g., the agenda behind the various parts of getting dressed).

> **Ascribing motives to others:** Working with the child to enable him or her to read what others say and do as expressions of their intents (e.g., understanding that particular intents underlie certain behaviors).

4. The Physical Context

Naive versions of children's language learning depict children's first words as names for what is in their immediate physical context. In this first naming stage, children are seen as building a concrete vocabulary. From there the children learn to combine words, as well as develop a vocabulary less dependent on what they are currently experiencing. It is said to be a stage of talk related to the "here and now" and to be the product of children making associations between what they see and what they hear.

In this association theory, words are taken to be associated with things, and word meanings are seen as associations between words and things (or an internal recollection of the external objects). Several elements are missing in this rendering of first words and their meanings. It does not consider the use to which words are put. Second, it fails to account for how objects are classified into categories. And, finally, it does not depict how objects are understood differently depending on what is going on in the situational event.

The pragmatics approach depicts children's first words as highly contextualized, not just by virtue of being tied to physically present objects, but by virtue of being tied to the child's current goals and affect and to the accompanying social and event contexts. They are referring expressions, not unlike the predications described by Grace de Laguna — expressions of feeling, social knowledge, and event knowledge, as well as knowledge of the presenting objects (de Laguna, 1927/1963). It is this larger sense of the role of the physical context that governs pragmatically based intervention — even that intervention having to do with "teaching first words."

Although the situated pragmatics approach to language intervention deemphasizes the traditional role that physical context is assigned in language learning, it does not discount the importance of physical context for supporting language learning. **Physical objects** become focal in children's evolution as they come to understand the world around them, and **physical space** provides children with schema for representing their world spatially. Both aspects of children's physical knowledge thereby offer children a basis for language and social learning.

5. The Event Context

Early this century Malinowski described how everyday events served as customs; how they conformed to rigid dictates in their execution; and how they served important cultural functions (see Chapter 1).

"Events" were rediscovered late in this century by those developing pragmatics intervention. The theoretical parents of event-based interventions are typically identified as Jerome Bruner and his colleagues (Bruner, 1977; Bruner & Sherwood, 1976), who studied regularities in the social games played by middle class British mothers and their infants, and Schank and Ableson (1977), who theorized that mentally represented scripts were part of the conceptual apparatus of intelligent humans (and machines). Event-based pragmatics interventions have recently been developed to help children understand and communicate in the events that comprise their daily lives (Constable, 1986; Culatta, 1984, 1994; Duchan, 1991; Snyder-McLean, Solomonson, McLean, & Sack, 1984; Sonnenmeier, 1994). Other interventions have taken events as an activity context in which to teach language structure (Bricker & Cripe, 1992).

6. The Discourse Context

Bakhtin was among the first to emphasize the influence of discourse context on language use. In 1952–1953 he wrote an essay on "The problem of speech genres" (reprinted and translated in Bakhtin, 1986) in which he illustrated how sentences are interpreted differently in different genres and how the genres have unifying and typifying characteristics which make them recognizable.

Bakhtin proposed that **discourse genres** contain within them a number of subgenres. A conversation, for example, could have a number of genres within it, such as greetings, question-answer exchanges, and proverbs. Current renditions of genres are broader than Bakhtin's. In today's parlance, Bakhtin's genres might be called exchange structures (Mehan, 1979) or adjacency pairs (Schegloff, 1968). Types of genres in today's broader scope have included conversation, event description, stories, expositions, and lessons.

Some language intervention approaches have been developed to teach children the features of different discourse genres (e.g., Brinton & Fujiki, 1989); others have been developed to use discourse as a context to teach other things, such as linguistic forms, vocabulary, semantic relations, or targeted speech acts (Constable, 1986; Culatta, 1984).

Whatever the genre, the language within it needs to be interpreted in ways that make sense. **Discourse coherence** includes the various ways those creating and interpreting discourse see it as a unified text. For example, all genres of discourse are likely to require an interpreter to keep track of the participants or objects being referred to and the spatial and temporal locations of the events being described (Duchan, Bruder, & Hewitt, in press). Interpreters create deictic coherence as they read or hear a text by creating a mental representation of characters or objects that populate the discourse and the point of view from which the depiction is expressed, as well as the spatial, temporal, and causal relations between the elements of the discourse. Interpreters, at any point in their hearing or reading of a segment of discourse, can tell whose viewpoint is being depicted and where and when in the text world the events are taking place (Bruder, in press; Segal, in press). Even very young interpreters can understand that the deictic term "I" in a narrated story is often a character in the text and that "here" and "now" refer not to the time and place of the storyteller, but rather to the time and place in the narrative where the events of the narrative are occurring (Duchan, in press).

◼ SUMMARY

The six domains identified as influencing and being part of communication have been put forward as pivotal areas for organizing language intervention programs. Most have already become focal areas for planning pragmatically based intervention approaches. Others, such as emotional context have yet to be explored. All of the domains need to be further understood and developed theoretically as well as clinically. The next two chapters treat the domains and their relations in more detail.

Social, Emotional, and Functional Contexts

The situated pragmatics approach to intervention calls for the provision of social, emotional, and functional support. Offering various types of support can help children better understand aspects of their social, emotional, and functional worlds, as well as provide support for them to better attend to other areas of learning.

◼⌐ THE SOCIAL CONTEXT

There are at least five ways children's social development has been studied and evaluated in the clinical and research literature. The first has been to examine which roles the children assume in different social interactions, the second to determine the diversity of roles played by the children, the third to find out how fully the children assume the roles assigned them, the fourth to look at how children tailor their communications to their partners, and the fifth to see how they participate in peer interactions. We will treat each in turn and discuss some methods developed for each that can provide children with the social support they need.

Role Relations

Social role relations vary with different cultures. Children in some cultures assume a central role of importance, and are thus able to play a dominant role in many of their daily events. These cultures could be said to be "child-centered." In other cultures, children are expected to be seen but not heard, and thus find themselves in more passive role relations when engaged in their daily routines. Thus, one factor influencing children's social participation is governed by the culture's assignment of their roles. Further, the same child in a particular culture will behave differently depending on what roles are called for on different occasions. The child may assume a role of submissiveness in a classroom interaction and a role of dominance in a dyad in which he or she holds the power (Domingo, in press).

Events also dictate role identities and relations, as evidenced by participants vying for who plays what role. Social relations will vary depending on whether the child is enacting the role of the father or mother, clerk or customer. Some events allow for role flexibility as is seen when children playing out a particular role negotiate for more power or when children are regularly assigned to roles that underestimate their abilities.

Role Diversity

While role relations may vary with the culture, the event, and the power relations between participants, one can see commonalities for some children in the roles they are assigned irrespective of contexts. These children, often those who are diagnosed with a disability, have been said to be cast in restrictive roles (Stryker & Statham, 1985). For example, in the 19th century children who were deaf were cast in roles that presumed they were incompetent and thus were not able to participate in events that allowed them power or to show their abilities. Currently, some children with severe communicative disabilities have been indicating through a new means of communication that they, too, have been underestimated, and thus disempowered (Biklen, 1993). Empowerment can be seen as a part of the language intervention process, with the emphasis here being on increasing role diversity.

Role Distance

Creating role diversity for children involves more than a mere assignment and more than supporting children as they assume their responsibilities in their assigned roles. For roles to be meaningful, children must identify with them. In his essay on role distance, Goffman asked how attached an individual is to an assigned role (Goffman, 1961) and differentiated the self assigned by the role from the individual self. The term "role distance" describes individuals who are assigned a role, but who wish to distance themselves from the identity prescribed by it.

Role Reciprocity

Besides constraining how a child may think about his abilities and about how to engage in life activities, an understanding of social roles offers the child a way of construing what others in the interaction are doing and thinking. Bruner (1977) and Snyder-McLean et al. (1984) have discussed how important it is for a child to understand the social role assumed by their partners during an interaction. This notion of others' roles, called role reciprocity, will vary with the social roles being played out (doctor vs. patient, teacher vs. student, mother vs. daughter) as well as the idiosyncrasies of the individuals playing the roles.

Evidence for young children's attunement to role recriprocity is found in the language of children as young as 4 years old who design their talk to fit their audience. They speak "baby talk" to their younger siblings and use a different register when talking to peers, older children, or adults (Sacks & Devin, 1976). For children to achieve positive social interactions, they now need to learn what motivates the behavior of others and how to respond accordingly.

Peer Relationships

Finally, the peer relationships among children in group contexts will affect the social interactions that take place in those contexts. Some children may be excluded by peers from activities or social interactions, and as a result the excluded child may not want to participate in those activities. An intervention program designed to have the child initiate and maintain social involvement with others may not be successful in these cases of social ostracization. (See Paley, 1994, for a sensitive discussion of this problem.) Programs have been designed to work with peers to achieve social acceptance for a child, thereby creating the groundwork needed for a child to become a member of a social group.

There is always the chance that these judgments of children's abilities underestimate their true abilities. Children are thus miscast in social roles that they may fail to identify with. Worse yet, they may take these roles as their true identities, as would be predicted by Mead and his followers in the tradition of symbolic interactionism. They may, for example, behave as if they were retarded, and not realize their true competencies. (See the comment of a facilitated communicator below as an example of this confusion.)

Facilitated Communication at Work

Kinney drugs is totally regular to me at work. It is different from the way I was treated other places.

In school they treated me like I was retarded. It made me feel retarded. At Kinney Drugs they make me feel proud of myself. They make me feel intelligent going to work each day at Kinney drugs.

F.C. helps me to talk to others at my job. Typing at work helps me to talk to others. I can let people know how I feel about them. I can ask people things that I could not ask help for before. Typing helps me to like my friends just like the other guys. I thought that I was retarded until I could type. Now I think that I am smart . . . .

> Tracy Thresher, a facilitated communicator,
> expresses his appreciation to those in his
> workplace for treating him as competent
> (from Thresher, 1992, p. 1)

What now needs to be developed is a means of identifying contexts in which children are underestimated by their interactants and changing the interactions so that children are cast in roles that are more in keeping with their level of competence. The next section provides suggestions for supporting children's social competence as they engage in interactions at school with their peers.

Providing a Supportive Social Context

Shifting from a deficit to a **competence view** of the individual is a crucial part of what is needed to develop supportive social contexts for the child. In the box that follows, Goode (1992) describes both positive and negative views of an individual with Down syndrome.

> Nowhere was Bobby discussed in terms of his having any sort of competence and human value; instead an exclusively fault-finding perspective was employed. The descriptions pointed to a series of encounters in which clinical standards of normality had been used as criteria to identify the consitutional faults of the client. The unintended but functional effect of this predominantly diagnostic outlook was to portray Bobby as essentially incompetent and hopeless.
>
> (Goode, 1992, p. 200)

After observing and interacting with Bob, and after studying interactions he had with others using videoanalysis, Goode found that Bob had considerable social savvy, and that he responded quite differently depending on whether his interactants saw him as "a case" of Down syndrome or as an individual with competencies and a distinctive personality.

> **Two Views of Bob**
>
> It was possible and valid to see Bobby as merely "a case" of Down Syndrome or as a person, if judged by normal standards, with a host of related problems. But it was equally valid and in most contexts more beneficial for Bobby to see him as a man with an unusual countenance and different ways of thinking and evaluating, trying to explore and master his everyday world. The humanistic basis of such a description, too often absent from clinical evaluations, directed our attention away from a client's deficits — from the ways he was different from us — and toward a person like ourselves who happened to have deficits in some areas and skills in others. Our experiences with Bobby showed that such a change was plausible and to the benefit of all concerned.
>
> (Goode, 1992, pp. 210–211)

It follows from Goode's discussion, that a major effort of intervention for many individuals should be to **create positive role relations** for them and **develop positive expectations** of them. These areas of endeavor involve providing support to those who are underestimating a person's abilities to help them change their regard and treatment of that person. One approach to this has involved a form of **sensitivity training** in which adults are made aware of aspects of their interaction styles that cast children in restrictive roles. Some of the activities that might be considered as part of the training are provided in Table 3–1.

A second avenue for supporting children's role development is to create **diverse role relations** for them. The roles can be assigned as jobs to be carried out as individuals in a group as is done in classrooms based on the collaborative model (Hill & Hill, 1990; Johnson & Johnson, 1987; Sharan & Sharan, 1992; Slavin, 1990). These classrooms are organized so that children work together to solve assigned problems, and thus learn in an interactive, noncompetitive way. Lieberman and Michael

TABLE 3-1
Dos and Don'ts for Helping Adults Improve Their Regard for Children with Disabilities.

Do: look directly at the child when you address him.

Do: include the child in activities even if he or she is not able to fully participate.

Do: offer the child choices.

Do: include the child in life decision making.

Do: enjoy the child, creating interactions that are not all serious.

Do: use language that is age-appropriate when talking to the child.

Do: work with the child in trying to figure out what to do about problem behaviors.

Do: avoid power trips or confronting tactics.

Do: interpret unusual behaviors in positive ways.

    BUT

Don't: talk about the child to others in his or her presence unless he or she is included in the conversation.

Don't: talk down to the child.

Don't: assume that problem behaviors are all intentional or under the full control of the child.

Don't: require that the child look at you before you continue the activity.

(1986) have applied the methods of classroom collaboration to group collaboration in speech-language therapy groups. They assign the children receiving language intervention role responsibility to carry out group activities and to evaluate the success of individuals in the group. The collaborative model includes assignments that provide children with a variety of roles, thereby offering them practice in carrying out different roles. Suggested roles (Flaherty, 1993; Hill & Hill, 1990), which are assigned and rotated for different activities on different days, could include:

1. *Leader:* Leads the activity, gets it going, and keeps it moving.
2. *Observer:* Watches the group and gives feedback. The observer rarely intervenes.
3. *Summarizer and reporter:* Writes down the main ideas and reports them.
4. *Encourager:* Provides encouragement and positive feedback to others. Asks people for their ideas.
5. *Clarifier:* Explains confusions, links ideas, asks for clarification.
6. *Checker:* Keeps people on track, reminds people of their roles, mediates disagreements.
7. *Challenger:* Stirs up thinking, takes a different point of view.
8. *Time-keeper:* Watches time, tells when time is nearly up.
9. *Questioner:* Forms open-ended questions for the group.
10. *Predictor:* Asks the group to predict possible outcomes of the project.

Another approach to teaching children to diversify their social roles is through pretend enactment of different roles. This approach is sometimes called scripted play (Sonnenmeier, 1994), socio dramatic play (Culatta, 1984, 1994; Goldstein, Wickstrom, Hoyson, Jamieson, & Odom, 1988), or role play (Bedrosian, 1985).

Children's ability to assume the role of a character in their pretense — or even in their life experiences — will depend on the fit between that character and their own role identities. Some roles, for example, one in which the child enacts a child patient in a doctor-patient scenario, are likely to be close to the child's life roles. Others, such as a doctor role, are different from what the child would experience. The box below includes descriptions made by Goffman of 3-, 4-, and 5-year-old children who have different takes on the role they assume as riders of a horse on a merry-go-round. Goffman, through this example, explicates his concept of role distance wherein some players may regard what they are doing as compatible with their personal sense of self and another; others may need to play the role with less investment of personal identity. The examples represent how roles must fit children's personal identities and understandings in order to be fully embraced.

Children's Role of Horseback Riders
on a Merry-go-round

At three and four, the task of riding a wooden horse is . . . a challenge, but apparently a manageable one, inflating the rider to his full extent with demonstrations of capacity . . . The rider throws himself into the role in a serious way, playing it with verve and an admitted engagement of all his faculties. Passing his parents at each turn, the rider carefully lets go one of his hands and grimly waves a small hand or blows a kiss — this, incidentally, being an example of an act that is a typical part of the role but hardly an obligatory feature of it. Here, then, doing is being, and what was designated as a "playing at" is stamped with serious realization . . .

To be a merry-go-round horse rider (at five) is apparently not enough, and this fact must be demonstrated out of dutiful regard for one's own character. Parents are not likely to be allowed to ride along, and the strap for preventing falls is often disdained. One rider may keep time to the music by clapping his feet or a hand against the horse, an early sign of utter control. Another may make a wary stab at standing on the saddle or hold on the post with one hand and lean back as far as possible while looking up to the sky in a challenge to dizziness. Irreverence begins and the horse may be held on to by his wooden ear or his tail. The child says by his actions: "Whatever I am, I'm not just someone who can barely manage to stay on a wooden horse." . . . This pointed separateness between the individual and his putative role I shall call **role distance** . . . The individual is actually denying not the role but the virtual self that is implied in the role for all accepting performers.

(Goffman, 1981, pp. 106–108)

Role reciprocity is yet another area of social awareness that comes into play as children develop. Role reciprocity has to do with ways children understand the roles of others in relation to the roles they themselves are playing. To understand why others do what they do, children need to have a sense of what to expect of others in the contexts of the social situations being played out. In nonpretense situations, children learn the roles of others as they engage in everyday life situations. A crucial aspect of script learning is to learn who the players are, what they usually do, and why they do it. A waitress who approaches is likely to offer menus or take an order, a gas station attendant is likely to fill the tank and needs to be paid (Duchan, 1991). Language intervention based on scriptal demonstrations can help children come to understand the differences in how participants respond in different situations, and facilitate their learning of role reciprocity. Classrooms based on collaborative learning contexts also can provide children with a new appreciation for how different participants assume different roles.

A fifth focus of support to help children engage positively in social interactions is to **actively promote successful interactions with peers**. Teachers may do this by designing contexts of success for an ostracized child, by creating friendship groups with children who are likely to get along, by emphasizing and publicly rewarding the competencies of a difficult child, or by helping the marginal child change in ways that will foster greater social acceptance.

Elaborate plans for creating peer support systems have been carried out by Marsha Forest, Judith Snow, and Jack Pearpoint from Toronto's Center for Integrated Education and Community. These service providers advise creating a network of friends, a "circle of friends," for children or adults with severe disabilities The circles help the person with a disability, called "the focus person," achieve life goals and create a network of people who provide the focus person with ties to their community (Mackan & Cormier, 1992). The adult, or facilitator, helps the circle of friends get established and keeps it active if it begins to falter. Below is an example of how to develop and use a circle of friends to achieve classroom inclusion for a child who has severe disabilities.

Developing a Circle of Friends
to Support Classroom Inclusion

Sometime just before or after the new student arrives, the facilitator invites the class members to join the new circle. The first meeting begins with telling the story of the new student in a way that helps her to talk about her dreams. The children will respond with suggestions about how

(continued)

> they can do things together and what problems they expect to encounter. The facilitator should encourage them to carry out these projects, and support their own problem solving. The facilitator needs to be in touch with the natural rhythm of the circle, helping it to meet as often as necessary to foster mutual support and relationships. At the same time meetings should not be overly formalized, and a simple get together at lunch time is often sufficient. Above all help the children to get a sense of when and how their meetings should be conducted . . .
>
> When the time comes to build a new curriculum for the new student, the students of the circle have become the experts who can tell the teachers, parents, and principal a great deal about what will work and what their friend has to offer, and gain from participating in the life of the classroom.
>
> (Snow & Hasbury, 1989, pp. 45–46.)

Finally, Vivian Paley has developed approaches for preventing social marginalization of children who are different. Her major theme is to create in school classrooms an atmosphere of social responsibility in which children abide by the social rule: "You can't say you can't play" (Paley, 1990, 1992, 1994). Paley works toward her objective in two ways. First, she creates a classroom in which children relate their feelings, ideas, and plans through stories. Within this story atmosphere, Paley creates heartfelt connectedness among the children, providing them with ways of understanding and accepting one another — what she describes as "drawing invisible lines between the children's images" (Paley, 1990, p. xi).

Paley's second approach to connecting students is to legislate acceptance — to make a rule that children cannot be ostracized, and to discuss the implications of the rule with her children to help them arrive at a moral consciousness that prevents them from excluding children from their interactive groups. Paley takes this heavier handed approach with trepidation (Paley, 1992). She asks: "What are the inherent educational justifications for placing such matters of fairness above friendship and free choice?" Her answer is that in allowing children to be ostracized we not only limit their learning potential, but also limit the learning of those who are doing the excluding (Paley, 1992, p. 17; 1994).

**Examples of Vivian Paley's Response
to Her Children When They Exclude
Someone from Their Play**

"Something unhappy took place today in the blocks." I tell
the children at rug time . . . "I couldn't decide what to do
about Clara's unhappiness."

I have everyone's attention. Like me, they yearn for
explanations of sadness . . . The children look at Clara to
see if she is still sad. "A lot of you," I continue, "think the
teachers always know what is right, but this time I don't
think the fair thing was done. You see, Clara was made to
feel unwanted. Not wanted."

(Paley, 1992, p. 13)

The following list summarizes the techniques developed for promoting peer relationships:

1. **Redirection of social overtures.** Having children direct their
   social overtures to other children, rather than to adults (Rice,
   Wilcox, Hadley, & Schuele, 1993);
2. **Elimination of socially penalizing behaviors.** Identify behaviors that interfere with social interaction and work with the
   child to eliminate them or to substitute a more conventional
   behavior (e.g., Gallagher & Craig, 1984);
3. **Peer acceptance by typical peers toward those with disabilities.**
   Work with peers to create contexts and attitudes of acceptance
   toward those with disabilities (Odom & Strain, 1984);
4. **Social skills training for those with disabilities.** Teach children
   with disabilities more socially acceptable behaviors such as
   sharing, resolving conflicts, responding to others' overtures
   (Goldstein & Gallagher, 1992);
5. **Create environments where nonacceptance is not allowed.**
   Work directly with children to help them understand and recognize the negative impact of being ostracized and to appreciate the worth of one another (Forest & Pearpoint, 1992; Paley,
   1990, 1992, 1994; Pearpoint, 1991; Snow & Forest, 1988).

■⬚ THE EMOTIONAL CONTEXT

The role of emotion in learning must certainly be greater than the attention currently being paid it. The research literature on emotion or affect has revealed a variety of ways that children are likely to learn about communication using emotion as a context for organizing their learning. The following four methods are suggestive when designing intervention programs that are sensitive to children's feelings and sense of self-esteem: affect attunement; social referencing; empowerment; and maintaining face.

Affect Attunement

Daniel Stern, in his influential book on children's acquisition of various representations of the self (Stern, 1985) has included **affect attunement** as a crucial way that adults can communicate with infants. Attunement includes not only tuning to the child's feeling states, such as anger and excitement, but also tuning to the child's "emotional vitality," which involves such things as surges in behavior and rhythmic duplications. Stern notes that the feeling state need not be responded to with a direct imitation of the original, but rather with an imitation of the feeling tone of the original. For example, the timing and excitement of vocalization by the child might be replicated in the head movement in the adult. The lack of direct imitation is Stern's evidence that the response of the adult is to the feeling tone of the child, an instance of affect attunement, and not to the form or content of the child's expression (see below for specific examples).

Examples of Affect Attunement

A nine-month-old girl becomes very excited about a toy and reaches for it. As she grabs it, she lets out an exuberant "aaaah!" and looks at her mother. Her mother looks back, scrunches up her shoulders, and performs a terrific shimmy with her upper body, like a go-go dancer. The shimmy lasts only about as long as her daughter's "aaaah!" but is equally excited, joyful, and intense . . .

A nine-month-old boy bangs his hand on a soft toy, at first in some anger but gradually with pleasure, exuberance,

---

> and humor. He sets up a steady rhythm. Mother falls into
> his rhythm and says, "kaaaa-bam, kaaaa-bam," the "bam:
> falling on the stroke and the "kaaaa" riding with the pre-
> paratory upswing and the suspenseful holding of his arm
> aloft before it falls.
>
> (Stern, 1985, p. 140)

There are three intervention programs which rely on what Stern
has called vitality qualities. Two are highly interactive, and could be seen
as being examples of affect attunement. Reun VanDijk's program for interaction with children who are deaf and blind involves a resonance
phase of interaction in which the adult and child move together (reson-
ate) in rhythmic, rocking movements. The adult then stops moving and
waits for the child's reaction. Resonance is achieved when the child follows the start and stop patterning of the adult (Stillman & Battle, 1984).

David Goode (1979) also developed a way of interacting through
movement with a child, Chris, who was diagnosed as deaf and blind and
severely retarded. Goode's technique involved what he called "meeting
Chris on her own grounds" (1979, p. 385). By remaining passive, Goode
allowed Chris to organize the activities. The following describes the first
occasion of his interaction with Chris.

> **David Goode's Notes on His First Interaction
> with His Friend Chris, a 9-Year-Old Child
> Who Was Diagnosed as Deaf, Blind, and Retarded**
>
> Chris maneuvered me in such a way that she was lying on
> my lap face up and had me place my hand over her face. By
> holding my hand she eventually maneuvered it in such a
> way that my palm was on her mouth and my index finger
> was on her right ("good") eye. She then indicated to me
> that she wanted me to tap on her eyelid, by picking my
> finger up and letting it fall on her eye repeatedly, smiling
> and laughing when I voluntarily took over this work as my
> own . . . While I tapped Chris's eye, she licked and sniffed
> my palm occasionally and softly hummed seemingly melod-
> ic sounds. We did this for about ten or fifteen minutes.
>
> (Goode, 1979, p. 388)

Miller and Eller-Miller (1989) and Miller and Miller (1973) have designed an intervention program in which the child is encouraged to develop movement spheres (repeated and rapid movement through tunnels, down slides, across elevated balance beams), to become attached to the repetitive activities, and then to have the momentum interrupted so the child is motivated to communicate the wish that the movement be continued.

Social Referencing

In addition to insights from the literature and intervention programs on affect attunement one can find a smaller but just as promising literature on children's learning to communicate affect by engaging in social referencing (Walden, 1993). This sort of referencing occurs in contexts of uncertainty and involves a naive observer checking out the affective reaction of a more experienced person for his or her reactions to what is going on. If the experienced person responds positively to, say, a stranger, then the learner is more likely to respond positively on subsequent occasions. The learner has thus determined through intentionally or unintentionally communicated emotional reactions of another person how to regard the new event.

Walden (1993) has argued from her literature review and logic that the ability to reference based on another's affect requires from the learner: (1) the ability to keep from responding to the unusual event until he or she checks with the knowledgeable observer; (2) the ability to engage in joint attention; (3) the ability to understand that expressions can "map onto objects;" and (4) the understanding that one can infer internal states from facial expressions. Social referencing also requires that the knowledgeable observer be able to provide relevant expressions of affect when the learner needs it.

Walden (1993) has carried out and reviewed several studies that have identified children who do not rely on social checking to alleviate their concerns about strange situations. Her conclusion is that children and mothers be trained on tasks of mutual attention. The feedback that children can get from their environment can offer them not only information about which aspects of their contexts are safe and dangerous, but also the information about the importance of affect expressions in everyday communications.

Maintaining Face

One powerful influence on children's social awareness is how they are regarded and evaluated by others. Children who do not behave in what is seen as "typical" or "desirable" ways may be treated atypically. Professionals are likely to consider such children as atypical, to classify them into a disability category (learning disabled, pragmatically impaired), and regard what they do as either positive or negative, given what would be expected for someone with that disability. Peers also create evaluative contexts for children who violate their expectations and may repeatedly ostracize selected classmates and place them in situations where they must make bids for acceptance. For these marginalized children, saving face is a continual issue. These children can but hope that they will be able to get through their daily lives without feeling embarrassed. One child expressed it as "Let's try to make it a good day" (Hood, McDermott, & Cole, 1980).

Eriks-Brophy and Crago (1993), in their study of classroom interactions among the Inuit, revealed a cultural dynamic that allows children with language learning problems to "maintain face." Unlike the dynamics in classrooms in the United States, the Inuit teachers do not call on particular children but instead address their questions to the group. Nor do they evaluate individual children's performances directly. If a child provides a wrong answer, the teacher models or repeats the desired response without making an overt evaluation of the child's incorrect answer. Children are encouraged to help one another and to find and correct their own mistakes. Eriks-Brophy and Crago recommend that the techniques of face building (rather than face reducing) of the Inuit be adapted for use in clinical and classroom interactions with children who have communication difficulties.

Another approach which has included affect in its intervention goals has been dubbed **affection activities** (McEvoy, Odom, & McConnell, 1992; McEvoy, Twardosz, & Bishop, 1990; Twardosz, Nordquist, Simon, & Botkin, 1983). These activities include prompts to the children to carry out actions of affection. For example, the children may be told to "hug a friend" or "give a neighbor a handshake." The researchers found that children trained in these procedures generalized them to free play settings.

■□ THE FUNCTIONAL CONTEXT — INTENTIONALITY

The most obvious and accepted idea about the functions of what appear to be children's communicative acts is that they are intended to communicate something to someone. When viewing acts as isolated from what else is going on in the situation, one has the impression that they can be analyzed as separate units, with little relation between them. That is to say, a request may be followed by another request, or by a response, whatever the communicator chooses to do. Further, the assumption is sometimes made that each act conveys a single intent, and only one intent. So a request for an object cannot, at the same time, be a bid for attention. (For an exception to this view, see Chapman, 1981 who discusses different levels of function for the same speech act.)

Examining what children do when first communicating, one finds that about 10 months, the typical child can convey intent, such as requesting by pointing to a desired object, and can convey a comment by showing an object to another. Later, the child comes to use language to request and comment. Assessment approaches have been designed to identify intents by looking at what the child does in the course of his communication. Children who carry out behaviors such as reaching or pointing are assumed to be performing the behaviors to accomplish a specified goal, to express a particular intent. (See Table 3–2 for a listing of such behaviors and associated intents).

From a broader and more situated view of intentionality, intent is seen as being embedded in what is taking place in the overall situation. In this view, the single act intents that are arranged to accomplish the same purpose are seen as related and as being a part of an overall **agenda** (Duchan, 1987; Lund & Duchan, 1993). Requests made during a game of fish, for example, are not whimsical but rather dictated by the event. They fall under an overall agenda to win the game by putting together the right combination of cards. The individual requests are not only individual requests for objects, but also part of a plan that is dictated by the rules of the game. In the box below Smith (1987) describes agenda as a fifth sense.

A Role of Agenda in Social Interaction

The fifth sense is a sense of the goal or objective to be accomplished. No matter what the relationship or setting, we do not use the same verbal and non-verbal behavior when we want to show interest as we do when we want to express disappointment. The objective may be very specific (e.g., to borrow money or to refuse to loan money) or more general (e.g., to make a good impression or to keep the conversation alive), but it must be kept in mind if we are going to achieve it. There are often multiple goals (e.g., to show concern for the feelings of the other while at the same time refusing a request), and sometimes conflicting ones (e.g., to show that we are all comrades but also to demonstrate that one person is in control).

(Smith, 1987, p. 4)

TABLE 3-2
Indicators, Types of Intents, and Means for Achieving Them as Manifested by Children in Their Earliest Stages of Communication.

Intents	Manifestations
Indicators (Bates, 1979)	Multiple phase movement (reach, grasp, lift) Dual focus — means and goal (e.g., person to get object, object to get person's attention) Change in effort when goal accomplished Change in means when goal is blocked Reaction of frustration when goal is blocked
Types of requests (Dore, 1975; McShane, 1980; Halliday, 1975)	Initiations requests for objects requests for actions requests for attention requests for information Comments labels objects comments on action Responses to other's initiations refusals protests answers repetitions acknowledgments
Means of achieving intents (Wetherby, 1991; Wetherby & Prizant, 1990)	Gestures, movements, gaze shifts giving showing pushing away pointing to a nearby object shaking head looking toward an object to achieve joint attention distal gestures (open-hand reaching, pointing at a distance, waving) unconventional gestures (banging an object to acknowledge its presence, looking at an object to request it) Vocal and verbal acts vocalizations to request, reject, etc. words to signify object implicated in intent (requested an object, noted object, name of person whose attention is requested)

Sources: Adapted from Bates et al. (1979), Dore, (1975), Halliday (1975), McShane (1980), Wetherby (1991), and Wetherby and Prizant (1990).

Single-act Intents

A variety of techniques have been developed in the clinical and research literature for promoting expressions of single-act intents. The most elaborated are a set of enticements for getting children to request objects or actions. Called **communicative temptations** (Wetherby & Prutting, 1984), the enticements involve situational setups designed to get children to want things and then to request them. Lids are put on too tight, desirable objects are placed out of reach, repetitive games are suddenly stopped, undesirable objects are offered, and so on. These sorts of efforts have been called **sabotage techniques** — the idea is to make something go wrong so that the child will request help in fixing it (Bricker & Cripe, 1992).

Various researchers and clinicians have proposed ways to support children's understanding and use of intents (Olswang, Kriegsmann, & Mastergeorge, 1982; Prizant & Rydell, 1993; Reichle, Halle, & Johnston, 1993). VanDijk (described in Stillman & Battle, 1984), suggested using boxes with objects in them to refer to components of the daily schedule (e.g., a rock from the playgound to suggest outdoor play time). The child can then request different activities, or change their sequence, by using the boxes to label them. (See the follwing box for some suggestions by these authors for aiding children in their developing single-act intents.)

Dimensions of Progression to Follow in Helping Children Improve Their Ability to Express Single-act Communicative Intents

1. Increase the different types of intents expressed (e.g., if child only requests objects, work on requests for actions).
2. Expand on the means child uses to express intents, increasing their variety and complexity (e.g., if child points, add vocalization; if child uses one word, help increase to two).
3. Provide child with means for referencing objects of intent (e.g., sequence boxes associated with daily activities to serve as a way to request those activities).
4. Convert unconventional forms to conventional (e.g., if child echoes part of an offer to indicate acceptance, provide him with a conventional acceptance phrase such as "Yes").

> 5. Convert socially unacceptable expressions of intent to more acceptable expressions (e.g., expression of rejection from crying to saying "no thanks").
> 6. Help a child to achieve an appropriate level of persistence if his or her intents are not responded to (e.g., encourage a reticent child to repeat requests or revise them, and not give up; encourage a child who is too persistent to abandon efforts if they are not attainable).
>   (After Wetherby & Prizant, 1985, and VanDijk as described in Stillman & Battle, 1984)

Other programs designed to facilitate children's use of single act intents have included teaching children to use Dore's (1975) nine primitive speech acts (Masters & Pine, 1992) or to work more specifically on eliciting and reinforcing particular intents, such as requests for actions, objects, and information (Olswang, Kriegsman, & Mastergeorge, 1982).

Children's ability to achieve their intents will also depend on the ability of their interactants to interpret them. A respondent who cannot understand a request will not be able to act on that request. Programs have focused on providing a child with a more interpretable means to **convey an already established intent**, rather than on eliciting a new type of intent. Children may have problems in conveying intents because they are unable to execute readable gestures or oral language. Some children express intents using echolalia (Prizant & Duchan, 1981; Prizant & Rydell, 1984, 1993), and partners unfamiliar with their communicative system fail to recognize their intent as such (Prizant & Duchan, 1981; Prizant & Rydell, 1984, 1993). Other children may use unconventional behaviors to indicate what they want (Donnellen, Mirenda, Mesaros, & Fassbender, 1984; Johnston & Reichle, 1993). Examples of approaches to help children convey their intents are outlined in Table 3–3.

Agendas

When intentionality is viewed as embedded in the event or discourse context, acts such as requests can be interpreted in their larger context. These, then, become part of the larger unit and no longer should be regarded as single acts, but rather as multiple acts serving a single purpose (i.e., an agenda). If, for example, one finds a context in which a child requests the same thing in a variety of ways, the different ways combine as ways to achieve an underlying agenda. In a discourse context, a

TABLE 3-3
Ways of Helping Children to Develop More Conventional Means for Conveying Their Intents. (A = adult; C = child; P = peer)

For immediate echolalia:
Respond to the assumed intent of the child's utterance (Prizant & Duchan, 1981)

> A: Do you want a cookie?
> C: Want a cookie?
> A: Here (give cookie to child under the assumption that the echo means "yes")

Provide the child with a model of the conventional language rendition of his utterance (Manning & Katz, 1989)

> A: Do you want a cookie? (to peer)
> P: Yes (takes cookie)
> A: Do you want a cookie? (to targeted child)
> C: Want a cookie?
> A: Yes? (offers a cookie)
> C: Yes (takes cookie)

For unconventional, rotely learned phrases:

Determine the fit between the rote phrase and the current context and provide a more conventional phrase to depict the same intent (Duchan, 1994b)

> C: Don't throw the dog off the balcony (said as he is threatening to push a glass of water off a table).

> A: Don't throw the glass off the table! (assumes that the phrase was originally learned in a context of throwing a toy dog off a balcony, and is now applied to situations of negative intent). (Example is taken from Kanner, 1943.)

For challenging behaviors that have social communication ties:

Determine which challenging behaviors occur in contexts where they seem to be serving a communicative function and substitute a conventional behavior or communicative act to achieve the same purpose (DePaepe, Reichle, & O'Neill, 1993; Johnston & Reichle, 1993).

> Challenging behavior = screams, attempts to bite, throwing objects.

> Contexts = (1) when he was asked to do something he didn't want to do (2) after having worked on a task for a period of time.

> Function = challenging behaviors associated with a desire to escape or obtain something.

> Substitute behavior = prompt a request to escape or to obtain a desired goal, stop the unwanted activity, or allow the person to leave the context before building up frustration (dubbed "safety signal intervention" by Johnston & Reichle, 1993).

lengthy monologue may be devoted to accomplishing a particular goal, as when a child makes an effort to persuade a parent that she should be allowed to go to the zoo with her friend. The single-act request "Can I go to the zoo?" is construed not as a single act, but as part of a larger persuasive genre "Mary's mother said she could go." "I haven't been for a long time." "I finished my work."

Similarly, clarification requests, sometimes viewed as single-act intents, often need to be viewed more broadly as part of an agenda. Unless viewed as such, they will not be fully understood. For example, confusions sometimes arise because of a misunderstanding about activity or something in the discourse genre. In these cases a request for clarification may occur after a period of confusion. Further, when a partner interrupts the forward flow of an interaction and raises a question about it, he or she creates a problem for both partners. The resolution of the problem often requires going beyond clarifying the immediately preceding communicative act. It may require locating a "trouble source" that occurred much earlier. Clarification requests are also likely to be followed by several exchanges before the repair is completed. Porter and Conti-Ramsden (1987) call these exchanges "loops." Finally, breakdowns caused by requests for clarification may lead to derailments and require an effort from the participants to get back on track.

The typical remedy required for such event or discourse breakdowns is that both partners need to work together to fix the problem and get to the project at hand as soon as possible. A repair may relate to a misunderstanding that occurred much earlier in an event, and the repair itself may continue for a while and require the work of both partners. Thus the agenda belongs to more than one participant and requires fixing the misunderstanding rather than clarifying something about the preceding utterance.

Techniques for Supporting Communicative Partners' Efforts to Achieve Their Agendas

Comprehension monitoring: Helping participants indicate when they do not understand something (Dollaghan & Kaston, 1986; Ezell & Goldstein, 1991).

Use of contingent queries: Helping partners better repair communication breakdowns (Brinton & Fujiki, 1989).

(continued)

Ethnographic interviewing: Determining the ways members of different cultures have of understanding what is taking place (Spradley, 1979; Westby, 1990).

Discourse analysis: Determining differences in partners' understanding of what is going on (e.g., Tannen, 1990).

■□ SUMMARY

This chapter has focused on three types of support children may need to communicate successfully in everyday life situations. The first, social support, includes helping them to understand their social roles and those of others. The second, emotional support, involves helping children interpret and convey expressions of affect and working to ensure that those in their lives maintain positive and empowering interactions with them. The third type of support, functional support, is aimed at helping children communicate their wants and needs as they participate in daily events and discourse contexts. Table 3–4 lists each of the three support contexts, along with a list of suggested things to do for each.

TABLE 3-4

Summary of Techniques for Providing Support Contexts in the Areas
of Social, Emotional, and Intentional Communications.

Support Context	Techniques
Social support	*Role diversity* — Use role play, scripted play, and cooperative groups, so that children have a variety of roles to draw from when experiencing the challenges of daily living.
	Role distance — Choose roles which children can embrace and which are in keeping with their personal identities, and expand on these roles while still keeping within the range of acceptable role identities.
	Role reciprocity — Help children understand their roles in relation to others in the context and to make sense of others' actions and discourse based on the goals dictated by the roles required for that context.
	Peer relationships — Engineer social contexts to get peers to interact; create a classroom culture that disallows ostracization and fosters friendships.
Emotional support	*Affect attunement* — In contexts that are affect laden, respond to the child's emotive content and mood.
	Social referencing — Provide children with social referencing in unfamiliar contexts to help them understand the affective import of those situations.
	Empowerment — Provide children with opportunities to engage in age-appropriate contexts and to take a positive and egalitarian role in carrying out the activities of those contexts.
	Maintaining face — Create contexts that are supportive and avoid those that are demeaning or embarrassing.
	Affect training — Create contexts in which children are expected to express affection toward one another.

(continued)

TABLE 3-4 *(continued)*

Support Context	Techniques
Support for intentionality	*Single act intents* — Respond to children's requests and provide positive feedback when they respond to yours.
	Agendas — Work with children to help them achieve event- and discourse-related goals.
	Ascribing motivations to others — Interpret the motivations of others to the child and model how the child needs to respond accordingly.

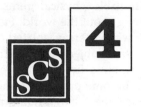

Physical, Event, and Discourse Contexts

When creating a support context for children who are learning to communicate, the supporter has a myriad of choices. Among the options are to manipulate elements from the physical context (e.g., objects, pictures, furniture, room changes), to design or highlight aspects of the selected events or activities, and to provide supportive discourse. This chapter will treat physical, event, and discourse support separately with the realization that their separation is artificial. Support can be provided in all three areas simultaneously during an actual communicative interchange. These contexts are also compatible with social, emotional and functional support discussed in Chapter 3.

■□ THE PHYSICAL CONTEXT

A situated pragmatics approach would involve using a learning environment similar or identical to that in the child's world of experience. It is in that everyday context that objects, pictures, and presenting action can provide concrete support for children's learning.

Physical Objects

Manipulable physical items, when contextualized, become props for learning about the world. Fisher Price toy firefighters along with a firetruck when seen as isolated elements are firemen and a firetruck. When these same objects are understood as props, they suggest a scenario for putting out a fire. Pictures of objects, when placed in the context of a story, become props for remembering what the story is about (Heath & Branscombe, 1986). Photographs of expeditions become mnemonics for remembering what happened. Objects given as presents at a birthday party take on added significance.

Different sorts of props vary in what they tend to elicit from children. Certain objects such as blocks, toy dishes, and clay have been found to promote social play; whereas other objects such as books, sand, and art materials tend to lead a child to solitary play (Charlesworth & Hartup, 1967; Rubin, 1977; Stoneman, Cantrell & Hoover-Dempsey, 1983; Van Alstyne, 1932). The use particular children make of objects can be studied to determine what those objects afford for those children. Objects that afford some children opportunities to interact with others may be used by other children for solitary play.

The following box illustrates the role of physically present objects in a child's description of the importance of provided objects in determining the course of her play.

**How a Child Uses Physically Present
Objects to Plan and Describe Her Future Play**

Doctor kit or nurse things. Well I could play listen to your heart, play x-ray and play blood pressure. I could pretend to look at somebody's finger. Well this is the easiest, look inside — then I'll figure it out. Play scissors for cutting nails. And play medicine. I use this tray. Nurse kit. They were supposed to give me a hat or an apron but they didn't give me a hat or an apron. Well, the nurse is in with the doctor thing and I mix them, sort of.

(Sutton-Smith, 1986, p. 195)

A clinician who is sensitive to opportunities offered by physical support would have in mind specific activities that the objects afford the child and would model or schedule activities in which the objects become meaningful — pictures are valuable in the contexts of stories, manipulative objects during pretend play. In other words, picture cards and toys become meaningful when they are made part of an activity by being introduced into an event of some sort. They, like words, need to be part of a larger context to become sensible.

Arrangement of Physical Space

Besides offering children manipulable pictures and objects, one can facilitate children's communication by creating interesting, suggestive spaces in a room. Accessible theme areas that are typical of preschool classrooms offer coherent physical space for suggesting and conducting different types of communication activities. Some common possibilities are: a kitchen with appliances, dishes, pots, and pans; a doll corner, with dolls, doll furniture, clothing, and a doll house; a section with different size blocks, tools; a book and tape area with books, headphones, soft chairs, rug; an art table with paints, colors, paper, easels; a water table with boats, floating toys; a sand box with shovels, water containers, molds for shaping the sand; a toy corner with riding toys such as buses, cars, trains; a small toy area with manipulable objects, sorted by theme; a puzzle area with puzzles of different levels of difficulty. Rooms used by occupational therapists are spaces that invite involvement of children. Although the goals of an occupational therapist are different from those of a speech-language pathologist, a team approach to service delivery might result in innovations in which the children's movement goals become coordinated with communication goals. (See the box below for an adaptation of Bricker and Cripe's [1992] suggestions for using movement activities to achieve communication goals.)

Movement Activities Designed to Achieve Communication Goals

The room may be divided into movement centers or a large space may be designated for all children to take turns at different movement activities. Materials such as beach balls or scooter boards can be arranged for designated areas or can be requested by children as needed.

Suggested Materials:

Balls, blankets, mats, scooter boards, water tub

(continued)

Possible Communication Goals:

Turns and looks toward person speaking.

Follows person's gaze to establish joint attention.

Requests or identifies object, person, and/or event (through gaze, pointing gesture, vocalization, or verbalization).

Engages in routine events with recriprocal turn taking and role enactments.

Sample Activities (using water tub):

Offer a tub without water, encourage child to ask for water.

If a child asks for water, pour a small amount in to encourage request for more.

Allow children to experiment with and discuss the physical properties of water.

Offer opportunities for trading items between children, modeling such requests.

Children can help with cleaning up — dumping the water into sink, drying the toys with towels, or hanging their aprons up to dry.

(Bricker & Cripe, 1992, pp. 193–194)

These regions in a room afford children opportunities and suggestions for how to become engaged with the world in various ways. The particular choices to be made depend on the children and their learning needs and interests. Sometimes selections can be fortuituous as was the case for educators who watched an 8-year-old child with autism change from repetitive activities to goal-related activities when he was met with a construction dig filled with large rocks.

The Usefulness of Climbing Terrains in Helping a Child with Autism Advance His Motor Planning

An 8-year-old autistic child, whom we had previously seen religiously rocking, stumbled across these rocks and soon began intently working his way from rock to rock across the ditch, where he would turn around and then return. The contrast between this child's encapsulated rocking

> and the goal-directed manner in which he crossed the
> ditch was striking.
> (Miller & Eller-Miller, 1989, p. 23)

■□ THE EVENT CONTEXT

What did you do in school today? Tell mom what happened yesterday?
Do you remember when we went to the zoo last week? Show me how to
build a house with these blocks. Let's play house. Such requests are often
encountered by children and require from them a conceptualization of
life's "stream of consciousness" into mental schemas which have typically been called events (Duchan, 1991; Nelson, 1986; Nelson & Gruendel, 1981). To describe or participate in an event children need to have
knowledge about their roles and those of other participants as well as the
action sequences and their temporal or causal relations (Duchan, 1991).
Also relevant is what Tharp and Gallimore (1988) have called the "when"
and "where" of events. That is, the child needs to know what contexts occasion the event. Finally the purpose or "why" of the event is important
in order to understand its function (Tharp & Gallimore, 1988).

Types of Events

An event type most often used in language intervention is the **structured
routine**. Routines are events, which are repeated and are recognized as
being the same when they recur. They tend to have little flexibility in that
repeated occurrences are likely to happen on similar occasions, with
similar props, with similar participants doing similar things. Helping
children learn routines can be thought of as teaching them the behaviors
required to carry out the routine (e.g., putting things away before moving to another activity). But the aim of intervention is best thought of as
providing the needed support so that the child understands not only
what to do but where new elements can be introduced and the significance the routine has in the larger setting of the classroom activities.

Routines can serve a variety of purposes: entertainment (e.g., hide
and seek, peek-a-boo), a way to interact with others (e.g., a greeting), and
a way to accomplish goals (e.g., a departure routine). They are part of
everyone's everyday life (routines of mealtime, bedtime, dressing, of
openings and closings of everyday events, religious rituals), and thus
provide an invaluable source for use in intervention.

Intervention based on routines is frequently carried out with children who are in the beginning stages of language acquisition. The programs involve supporting children in learning about aspects of events and, hopefully, helping the children to understand the function and occasions when the event is likely to be enacted (Snyder-McLean, Solomonson, McLean, & Sack, 1984; Sonnenmeier, 1994).

A potential problem with focusing intervention on rote routines is that children may memorize the elements and then become committed to the routine without being able to appreciate its conventional meaning or function in the culture (Fletcher, 1983). Kanner (1943) in his description of one of his clients with autism describes the boy as being quite upset when his routines were not literally followed.

Leo Kanner's Description of "Preservation of Sameness" in His Client Donald

A great part of the day was spent in demanding not only the sameness of the wording of a request but also the sameness of the sequence of events. Donald would not leave his bed after his nap until after he had said, "Boo, say 'Don, do you want to get down?' " and the mother had complied. But this was not all. The act was still not considered completed. Donald would continue, "Now say 'All right.' " Again the mother had to comply, or there was screaming until the performance was completed. All of this ritual was an indispensable part of the act of getting up after a nap.

(Kanner, 1943, p. 245)

Routines, by their nature, do not allow for flexibility. Events that have more room for creativity are "scripts." Scripts also require that the child know what is about to happen, what the parts of it are, and how the event functions, but scripts are more open-ended and less prescriptive than are routines. For example, a birthday party is a predictable event in that it usually takes place at a child's house, involves giving presents, blowing out birthday candles, and playing games (Nelson & Gruendel, 1981). However, particular parties may differ in their locations, presents, types of refreshments, and participants. Nelson and Gruendel have called these generalized representations of events **generalized event representations**. Pragmatists refer affectionately to these event representations as "GERs."

What to Support in Event Learning

Event comprehension, like reading comprehension or language comprehension, can range from elementary to sophisticated, and is likely to differ depending on one's experience with the elements being comprehended. Children may recognize the props in an event but not know how to use them. Or they may be able to enact one role, but not the recriprocal role. Or children may know how to sequence the steps in an event but not understand how the elements of the sequence are related or how they function as part of the overall event understanding. Or they may be committed to doing the event in a particular way and be inflexible when a new enactment requires change.

Intervention that helps children understand and carry out events will thus differ, depending on the comprehension needs of particular children. Children who have trouble understanding causal relations between action sequences or between motivation of characters and their actions need support events with elements that are causally related (e.g., packing a suitcase, planning what to take for a camping trip, figuring out what will happen given a set of circumstances). Children who are unacquainted with the rules of a game need experience with the game to be able to perform in it (e.g., Shultz, 1979). Table 4–1 lists some of the elements of events that can be the focus of the intervention, depending on the special needs of the children engaged in the event.

Ways of Supporting Event Learning

There is a developing literature on the use of the events in language intervention and a set of techniques which have been offered as ways to help children learn how to participate and communicate in different event contexts. For example VanDijk (Stillman & Battle, 1984) has recommended the use of "**sequence boxes**" containing objects that can be used as mnemonics for an activity (e.g., a spoon to signify snack time); and Snyder-McLean et al. (1984) have offered a structure for organizing lessons around "**joint action routines**," or "JARS," as a method of supporting children's learning of routinized events.

Features of Joint Action Routines

General Characteristics:
    1. Typical of activities that occur in children's every day lives;

(continued)

2. Are predicable
3. Are structured
4. Occur in known and established contexts

Types:
1. Activities which result in a final product (e.g., cake)
2. Activities with a story theme
3. Cooperative turn-taking activities

How to create or select joint action routines to work on:
1. Design it around a specified theme
2. Include a requirement for joint attention
3. Use a limited number of roles

TABLE 4–1
Aspects of Event Knowledge That Might Be Focused on in Intervention.

1. Who the participants usually are.
2. The social (power) relation between the participants.
3. The ascription of motivation to participants.
4. The actions prescribed for different participants.
5. The causal, temporal, or other relations between action sequences.
6. The goal (function) of the event as a whole.
7. The rules governing what is allowable (e.g., turn-taking rules for games).
8. The language usually used in the event.
9. When the event ordinarily takes place.
10. The cultural relevance of the event (e.g., birthday parties; gender restrictions — who does the cooking in that family/culture).
11. The significance of the objects used in the event (e.g., grocery stores sell food; getting dressed requires selection of clothes to fit the occasion; toys or objects may directly or abstractly represent other objects).
12. The spatial arrangement of people and objects (stores, learning centers).
13. Negotiating ability to assign roles, determine action, create innovations.
14. The ability to elaborate on known events and substitute new appropriate elements for old ones.
15. Event framing (how to move from real to pretense, how to get other children to participate).

One technique for facilitating event learning has been called a script approach (see Sonnenmeier, 1994), in which the "support person" presents the entire event to the child repeatedly, gradually fading support so that the child can take a part in the event's enactment. As the child is learning the event the supporter might need to provide occasional **prompts** to encourage and promote participation. Among the things the child needs to learn are role recriprocity, action sequences, the cultural and situational import of the event, and when and where it is enacted.

A commonly used way to support children in learning the events of a culture is to have them watch and in so doing act as apprentices until they feel comfortable engaging directly in the event. This method of **demonstration through observation** allows the future participant to become highly familiar with the routine without making errors (Lave & Wegner, 1991).

Once a routine is developed, it can be elaborated by **expanding on what is typically done** (Duchan, 1994b; Sugarman, 1984). For example, Sugarman suggested that repetitive routines typically performed by children be used to establish social interaction. She joined in one child's solitary routinized play, thereby elaborating on the role structure of the original routine. A second way of expanding on a known routine is to insert new elements into various slots of the routine. For instance, when enacting a grocery shopping routine, instead of having the cashier say a particular phrase, such as "May I help you," one can model a variety of things which might be said by a person playing that role. Third, routines can be expanded by including new participants, as is described in the following when a child who was on the periphery of a social activity was subsequently included.

Haring's Description of "Creating Social Niches"

In analyzing the social contact patterns of a kindergarten-age boy, it was found that he was attracted to a game on a playground slide. Interviewing some members of this group revealed that the game was called "slime monster," and the purpose of the game was for the boys at the bottom of the slide (the slime monsters) to pull boys at the top of the slide down. The boys were asked if the target student could be another slime monster with them during the free play period. For the next several days, the target student played with this group of boys without further need for intervention.

(Haring, 1992, p. 317)

If elements of different routines are similar in function or structure, they can be learned as **subroutines** and applied to new events in new contexts. A three-step object exchange routine (an object is requested, the object is given, and the requester thanks the partner) can be a subroutine in a variety of contexts (grocery stores, clothing stores, libraries). Schank (1982) has called these subroutines "memory operating plans," or MOPS, and has argued that these MOPS are much more versatile and offer more flexibility in understanding what is going on than the larger routines in which they are embedded.

For children who become overly committed to a particular version of an event, methods have been designed to help them develop **event flexibility**. For example, Simons (1974) designed approaches to children whom she called "compulsive" which included limiting the child's performance of a fixed and favored activity in one place at a particular time or recontextualizing an activity by using it in different ways throughout the day. Paley (1990) incorporated one of her student's helicopter play into the play of the other children to have his isolated activities become more socialized.

Once children are able to participate in frequently occurring events, and can use them in ways that fit the context specifications, the support person might progress to more **open-ended events**, in which the children must create new elements for the particular occurrence, such as is the case for a birthday party which offers the possibility for different participants, different presents, and so on.

Group problem solving is a method in which children with some knowledge of events might engage in developing a new version of those events or a deeper understanding of the elements of the event. For example, activities can be designed wherein the children talk together about what props might be needed for a particular open-ended event, say a picnic, and decide together where they will go and what they will do.

An Event-Based Curriculum

Following the tenets of Dewey (see Chapter 1), it is feasible to carry out an entire program of language intervention based on event learning. This approach can be implemented by the speech-language pathologist in concert with the classroom teacher and family members. The events selected for use should be ones that are functional in the life of the child, and they should be presented, wherever possible, in the context of ultimate use. Eating routines should be done at mealtime in the school cafeteria, for example.

Sometimes it is not feasible to assist the child's learning in the context of ultimate use. For example, we worked with one person with autism to prepare him for his bar mitzvah. In these cases, simulation of the ultimate contexts can be carried out, and the parts learned for the eventual real-life experience.

Care must be taken to ensure authenticity of simulated events that are used for practice outside contexts of ultimate use. There is a big difference between children playing with dolls in ways that simulate everyday life roles and events and teachers creating sorting activities in a sheltered workshop as a simulation of work activities. Simulation activities must be seen by the child as related to the ultimate activity, and as meaningful. Further, it is ill-conceived to focus solely on simulation activities without providing opportunities to use what is practiced in the "real world" context. Indeed, a situated pragmatics view would argue that children will have an easier time learning to carry out real-life activities in naturally occurring contexts than they would in practice activities where they must imagine how it would go in the real world. Table 4–2 presents some questions to be asked about a simulation activity that would allow one to gauge its authenticity and value.

TABLE 4–2
Judging the Authenticity of Simulation Events.

1. **How closely does the simulation event approximate the real world event?** Cardboard buses in classrooms used for mobility training may not be seen as the real thing.

2. **Is the simulation event meaningful to the child?** Activities that are broken into subparts may lose their meaningfulness. Taking off lids is meaningful only if the act functions to get what is inside. Reading maps is meaningful only if it is understood as a means for locating places or finding one's way.

3. **Does the child readily engage in the simulation activity?** Authentic simulation activities occur in children's creative play and are engaged in by choice. These are much different from imposed activities that children are required to engage in.

4. **When will the child be judged as ready to carry out the activity in the real world?** Waiting until the child achieves a prespecified level of competence with the simulation activity before engaging in the real-life activity may be ill-conceived, especially if the real-life activity is easier to do.

A curriculum of event training can be organized so that there is a logical progression for moving from one event context to another. Table 4–3 offers some ways that the program might progress as the individual becomes more competent in carrying out a particular event or a series of related events.

■ THE DISCOURSE CONTEXT

In event contexts, the participants are engaged in an activity, a happening, that involves more than talk or writing. Events usually have props such as food, clothing, or money and participants use the props to achieve a common purpose. Discourse, on the other hand, lacks props; or if there are props, they are ancillary to what is being accomplished. Conversations can take place in the presence of food, but the food is not "used" by the conversationalists to carry out their discourse. This distinction between event talk and discourse has been made as one of analytic convenience (Lund & Duchan, 1993). (Cazden [1979] made the same distinction, but called event talk "speech situation" and discourse "speech event.") There are likely to be events that are mostly talk, such as those involved in book reading; and there are likely to be sections of discourse that are related to the immediate context, such as a conversation between two cooks about the recipe they are using to prepare the meal.

Discourse Genres

Discourse comes in a variety of types which are distinguishable from one another by their organizational structure, their function, and participants' roles. The types, called discourse genres, that are most often emphasized are conversations, event descriptions, stories, expositories, and school lessons.

The type of discourse usually thought of as the quintessential genre is **conversational discourse**. Conversations have received the most attention from analysts and clinicians alike. Perhaps because it is seen as the most frequently used way of communication, many clinical programs see conversation as the ultimate goal of language intervention. In the past it has been equated with "connected speech," currently it is taken as a synomym for discourse.

The term "conversation," when interpreted more technically to mean one type of discourse genre, can be studied for its characteristic features. Most studied are dyadic conversations between equal partners.

TABLE 4–3
Graduated Dimensions for Selecting Events as Targets of Intervention or as a Support Contexts.

1. From events with a few steps to ones with many steps.
2. From everyday familiar to occasional unfamiliar.
3. From highly prescribed and routinized to open-ended.
4. From roles consistent with own life roles (e.g., customer) to ones that are incongruent (e.g., clerk).
5. From highly scaffolded to unscaffolded.
6. From contextualized to decontextualized
7. From high to low affect.
8. From real to fanciful.
9. From one to many logically related events (get ready, go out, come home, go to bed).
10. From one In a day to several In the same day (e.g., scheduled activities in school from morning arrival to first activity to mid-morning snack, etc.).

The function of the conversation is positive social exchange. When a conversation begins to be too one sided, or when the partners become agonistic, it turns into another genre such as "lecturing" or "arguing."

Conversations require that partners take turns in prescribed ways, and that the content of the talk be organized around a topic. Conversations can contain formatted exchange structures such as question-answer exchanges, but should not include questions that are tests of another's competence or evaluations of others' performances. When conversations begin to have many test questions and evaluations, they become more like lessons and lose the social and egalitarian quality that is characteristic of conversational exchanges.

Some children do not readily converse, and thus can be said to have conversational difficulties (Evans, 1987; Fey, 1986). Others may talk at the same time as their partners, showing insensitivity to the etiquette of conversational turn taking. Still others may have problems initiating or maintaining conversational topics or in repairing conversational breakdowns when they occur (Brinton & Fujiki, 1989).

Although conversations between two people have been given priority in assessment, intervention, and research, multiparty conversations often occur in children's lives, such as the one in the next box. This multiparty conversation took place in a kindergarten classroom just after the children had returned from the library. The librarian had told the children that if they listened quietly to her story they could make a wish that would come true "in a year and a day." Her promise bothered the kindergarten teacher, who felt that the children "were being tricked into good behavior."

Teacher:	I've never heard of making a wish after a fairy tale. I'm not sure I agree with the librarian.
Eddie:	It could happen because I lost a gorilla from my adventure set and I found it.
Jill:	Wishes do come true, you know.
Teacher:	But how does the librarian know they'd come true in a year and a day?
Wally:	See, one day she made a wish after listening quietly to a story and it came true in a year and a day.
Andy:	I made a wish that my daddy would bring me a toy from downtown and it did in one day.
Teacher:	What causes wishes to come true?
Jill:	Just by themselves or they're not wishes
Deena:	Fairies do it. It has to be fairies. I lost my library book and I wished I would find it and it came true in two days. That's because it was an easy wish.
Wally:	If the fairy is busy with teeth, Santa Claus might do it.
	(Paley, 1981, pp. 32–33)

Children are often asked to describe "what happened?" Their response, cast as an **event description**, is expected in mainstream American culture to be informative, objective, and factual. The description should include a description of the participants (if they are significant) and should tell what happened by organizing the relevant subevents in chronological order. The story told is supposed to be the truth, and unlike fictional stories what is said can be refuted. (For an exception to these truth-telling stories see Heath's [1983] description of those who tell boasting stories with a premium on the degree to which the tall tale departs from a plausible truth.)

In the extract below a 5-year-old typically developing child was asked whether her dog ran away. The child recreates an experience. Her event description borders on being a story in that it has intrigue and is told in a way so as to elicit suspense (e.g., "all of a sudden" in line 5).

1. I don't re . . . We had to call him, Fritz back.
2. He wouldn't come when we were calling him.
3. Cause he saw a real rabbit.
4. He couldn't find it.
5. And all of a sudden Jim went out in the back.
6. And Fritz came in. (Peterson & McCabe, 1983, p. 227)

Stories, sometimes referred to as narratives, are distinguished by having **emotional or entertainment value** (Brewer & Lichtenstein, 1982). Those that are structured around a plot often involve suspense deriving from a character's inability to achieve a goal. The suspense is released when the circumstances blocking the goal are somehow circumvented.

Some researchers have examined children's narratives and created intervention programs based on whether the children have organized their stories into what has been called a "story grammar" structure. Roth and Spekman (1986), for example, have assessed children's stories for the following components, basing their analysis on the work of Stein and Glenn (1979): (1) setting, (2) initiating event, (3) internal response, (4) plan, (5) direct consequence, and (6) reaction.

Researchers using story grammars as a guide to what children's stories should contain have typically judged the children's ability to recall elements in a story provided them. The template story, the one they are recalling, is usually created by adults for children, and is chosen by the researchers because it contains the six elements specified by the story grammar. However, many stories spontaneously created by children of different ages who are typical as well as atypical learners do not conform to the adult stories designed for children. The story below, for example, fails to conform to the elements of the story grammar, even though told by a typical 5-year-old who was selected by his teacher and classmates as a teller of enviably interesting stories. There is no plan, nor is there an initiating event that blocks a plan. The problem which creates the plot structure is established tacitly in the setting — the lion's loneliness, and is solved in the course of the story, but in unexpected ways.

1. Once upon a time there was a little lion
2. and he lived alone
3. because his mother and father was dead
4. and one day he went hunting
5. and he saw two lions

6. and they were his mother and father
7. so he took his blanket to their den
8. because it was bigger (Paley, 1981, p. 9)

Discourse is classified as **expository** when it is organized as objective information, providing facts to an audience that does not know those facts. Exposition is the mode for most of what is thought to be "scientific writing," in that it portrays information with unequivocal authority and from a third-person, objective point of view. The facts are supposed to rest on truth conditions which occur in the world. So, unlike for stories, information in expository discourse is testable against an outside truth; thus the information presented is refutable.

In the following extract a 5-year-old is responding to a request that he tell a story. Instead, he related some scientific facts couched in the language of exposition, along with a few sentences (the starred ones) that were his effort to respond, albeit minimally, to the request to tell a story.

1. When you pick up a piece of the moon and bounce it,
2. it goes down
3. and then it comes up.
4. Then it floats all around space
5. cause there isn't a single smidge of air.
6. On Jupiter you can live if you're in a space house.
* 7. There's a little boy there
* 8. and he cleans the space house.
* 9. Once in a while he puts on his space suit
*10. and shoots off a piece of the moon.
 11. Then there's rings all around Saturn.
*12. The boy looks at them
*13. and then he goes inside to look at them better.
*14. But they're just clouds.
 15. They're red hot pieces of rock
 16. and when they come in earth's atmosphere they make a big hole.
 17. Then Mercury is the hottest planet of all near the sun
 19. and your blood would boil.
*20. The boy just stayed on Jupiter
*21. and looked at things
*22. and once in a while a meteor came down.
 23. And Pluto has snow two hundred feet deep.
 24. And also the sun's light doesn't even have enough (to) light up outer space
 25. and the army sends up missiles to outer space to see what the weather is.
 26. They have a man who writes down the weather that's going on.
 27. Then some stars can whirl 'round and 'round.

28. When they break they make smaller stars,
29. and when they break they make dust.
30. There are two hundred rocket jets
31. and the middle has one hundred jets,
32. and the top rocket has ten jets.
33. And the hatch is in the earth's atmosphere
34. and a man can parachute down to the ground. (Pitcher & Prelinger, 1963, p. 116)

One of the ways school discourse has been portrayed as being different from home discourse is that there is a predominance of **lessons** at school. The term "lesson" can be seen as a description of a school event in which activities are carried out. This sense of lesson is a broad one, and is usually used to differentiate times of the day devoted to different subject matter: a reading lesson, a math lesson, an art lesson. More recently, lesson has been used to describe a particular type of event at school, one previously called "recitation" in lessons the teacher asks the students to perform, calls on one student to respond to a request, and evaluates his or her response for its correctness. This three-part exchange structure, referred to an an initiation-response-evaluation (IRE) exchange (Mehan, 1979), is repeated again and again, until time for the lesson runs out or the activity is accomplished.

Lessons function as a way to regulate the interaction when many students are involved. They have a prescribed turn-taking structure and are usually preplanned and orchestrated by the teacher (see Table 4–4).

Below is an example of what many would call a lesson. If one were to take the IRE structure literally, a conclusion might be drawn that this is an irregular lesson because it does not contain an evaluation after the children's responses. However, using notions embedded in schema theory, one could argue that the evaluation component is implied. That is, it is tacitly offered by the teacher and understood by the children. All participants make the assumption that when the teacher goes on to another child with a new question she regarded the response to the last question as correct. One might venture to guess that there may have been a head nod or other nonverbal indicator from the teacher (not captured on audiotape) that could be read by the children as a positive evaluation.

A telling example of the importance of discourse structuring is presented in the lesson example in the box below. At the end of the interaction, a child attempts to ask the teacher a question during the time she is providing instruction ("Should you write the word?") The teacher indicates her displeasure by "begging his pardon," probably intending the comment as a reprimand for his interruption, rather than actually asking for his pardon. The teacher's emphasis on managing the discourse is ironically displayed by her follow up of what she takes to be an interrup-

TABLE 4-4
An Exchange Sequence Which Has Been Seen as a Way Lesson Discourse Is Structured (e.g., Mehan, 1979).

Sequence	Description	Examples
Initiation	Teacher asks test questions,eliciting a response from a child or group of children; questions often framed to see whether they know the correct answer.	Who knows . . . ? Do you remember . . . .? Look at the top of the page . . .
Reply	Student replies by giving an answer.	*Question:* What kind? *Answer:* Subtype *Question:* What color? *Answer:* Color name *Question:* Yes-no question *Answer:* Yes answer
Evaluation	Teacher responds to student reply.	Acceptance (right) Direct correction (no, . . .) Soft correction (yes, but) Going on to next child Asking for self-correction

tion when the child asks a question too soon — she asks, shortly after the child has asked a question, whether there are any questions. The discourse of lessons is thus revealed; one needs to learn where in the structuring of the discourse that questions are allowed and where they are considered to be interruptions.

A School Lesson

Teacher: Would you look at the first picture please? It is a picture of a . . .

Class: Bed, bed, bed

Teacher: You will spell the word bed. All of the pictures on this page are spelled with a sha, with

	an eh sound. Like an eh or the ell sound. Let me read the pictures to you. Bed, nest
Class:	Nest
Teacher:	Let, ten, James is going to choose a book from the library that is by him and David's going to do the same, ten tent.
Class:	Tent
Teacher:	Elf
Class:	Elf
Teacher:	Wet
Class:	Wet
Teacher:	Steps
Class:	Steps
Teacher:	Sets
Class:	Sets
Teacher:	These are stars, but it's also a picture of a set, of three jointed to a set of two to make a set.
Student:	Should you, should you write the word?
Teacher:	I beg your pardon. To make a new set of five. Are there any questions about this? (Mac-Kay, 1974, pp. 227–228)

Discourse Coherence

Besides global level discourse genre features, a discourse also has elements that allow it to be coherent. The interpreter knows, for example, that a character, say a dog, when mentioned repeatedly in a text is the same dog. Very young children can track the main characters in a text, especially when they are conveyed through pictures in a book. So, participant tracking through repeated references to the same story characters offers the discourse its needed coherence.

Another strong contributor to discourse coherence are deictic elements in a discourse. Deixis has been interpreted in the past as confined to particular words which take their meaning from the context, such as personal pronouns (I, you), spatial terms (here, there), and temporal terms (now, then, yesterday). Discourse deixis has to do with the parts of the discourse that help the interpreter build a representation of the perspective, space, and time of the events being described. (See Lund and Duchan [1993] and Duchan, Bruder, and Hewitt [in press] for a more detailed account of discourse deixis.)

Although discourse deixis has yet to receive the attention it deserves from language interventionists, its influence is often felt. Clinicians who try to teach pronouns to children need to help them understand that these deictic terms mean different things depending on the time, place, and person uttering them. Also, spatial prepositions often present the clinician with deictic dilemmas. Anyone who has tried to teach a child sitting across the table to "put the apple behind the tree" experiences the realization that "behind" is interpreted in accordance with a given perspective, and what is "behind" for the child can be seen as "in front of" for the clinician, or "beside" to the bystander looking at the tree from another angle.

Providing Discourse Support

Children need to know different things about discourse depending upon the genre being targeted. Table 4–5 provides examples of what aspects of different genres may need to be targeted for intervention.

The elements listed in Table 4–5 differentiate the genres. It should be kept in mind, however, that it is commonplace to have a mixture of genres in the same discourse. A child may be telling a story and shift to a conversation or to expository (see the example on page 76). A teacher may be conducting a lesson and shift to a conversation in an effort to find the relevance of a point to a child's personal experiences. An event description may contain pieces of narrative from a well-known story. Indeed. Vivian Paley regularly brings story lines into her conversational exchanges with her students with the intent of bringing a well-known and more distant "landscape" to bear on current experiences (Paley, 1990).

Although there are notable differences between discourse genres, there are also similarities across genres. For example, all genres need to be initiated, and a legitimate target for intervention is to provide children, especially reticent ones, with ways to initiate or request the genre of their choice.

Children who tend not to initiate may have difficulty doing so because they lack a way of asking for what they want. The interventionist may provide the child with choices. The choices may be verbal (e.g., Do you want to tell stories or play house?) (Kirchner, 1991b) or pictures or object choices (sequence boxes based on the child's daily schedule as suggested by VanDijk, cited in Stillman and Battle [1984]).

TABLE 4-5

Global Structures and Functions to Target for Providing Support for Different Discourse Genres.

Structures	Functions to Target
Conversations	Conversational turn taking
	Topic initiation
	Topic maintenance
	Social function
	Repairing
Event descriptions	Causal relations
	Temporal relations
	Scriptal structure
Storytelling	Entertainment value
	Plot structure: episodes
	Evaluation
	Framing
Expository	Logical relations
	Unequivocal assertions
	Factual knowledge
Lessons	IRE exchange structure
	Interruption conventions
	Teachers' strategies for determining correct information

Children can be provided opportunities for engaging in discourse by virtue of **spatial arrangements** in the classroom and **time allocation** for certain activities. For example, a housekeeping corner can promote pretend conversations; Fisher Price play stations can promote play involving service encounters; sharing time can elicit event descriptions; story time or book time can elicit narratives; and an activity involving teaching peers how to do something is likely to promote event descriptions or expositions. **Suggestive props** provide children with support in initiations and enactments of discourse-based activities. For example dress-up clothes can suggest particular roles to be played out, and objects such as toy foods or dishes can give the activity some needed structure.

Transitions from one activity to another are likely to require **shifts in discourse**. Some children have difficulty following the shifts or in leaving one activity and getting ready for another. Various programs have suggested that **shift indicators** be used between activities. They serve to help children identify the need to finish one type of activity involving a particular sort of discourse and to begin another. Some teachers of young children have helped the children through transitions by instituting an intermediate activity such as songs or requiring children to put things away or get ready for a second activity (see VanDijk's use of sequence boxes, described in Stillman and Battle [1984] for an example of a shifting indicator). Teachers of older and more verbally facile children might more likely talk a child through a transition, explaining that one activity is ending and describing what is to happen next. For children who are literate, written schedules of daily events aid children in making event and discourse transitions.

Another area of discourse in which some children are likely to need support involves **discourse coherence**. Once involved in a discourse episode, children may lose interest or not have the resources to continue participating. The supporter may offer such a child a **prompt** or encouragement to continue. Some prompts are characteristic of a particular genre. For example, "one day . . . " can prompt a child to provide a move from a story setting to the main line of the story; "What happened then?" can promote the next event in a story or event description.

Supportive questions can also provide a structure for a child who has difficulty maintaining a discourse line. The following box shows how a kindergarten child was able to incorporate the questioning of her teacher into her own story line, and thus provide her own discourse support.

Five-Year-Old Rose's Use of Her Own
Verbal Scaffolding in Story Production

A girl said, "Can I go for a walk?" Who'd she say it to? Her mother. "Okay, you can go." She went to the forest and saw Squanto. Who's Squanto? An Indian. "Do you want to live with me?" Yes, she did. She asked could her mother come too? "Yes."

(Paley, 1981, p. 85)

Hewitt (1994) described a language intervention program she developed for a high school student with autism who tended not to create a subjective representation for characters in narratives. The student, prior to her intervention, did not understand that the wolf who dressed up as a grandmother was aiming to fool Little Red Riding Hood, nor did he understand that the child was deceived by the wolf as evidenced by the grandmother's refrains: "Why grandmother, what big XXs you have." Hewitt's intervention consisted of having **"meta" discussions** during and after reading stories. The discussions revolved around who was feeling or thinking what in the story.

The literature on pragmatic intervention has embedded in it a host of techniques that offer the child support at the local level of discourse coherence. (See Duchan and Weitzner-Lin [1987] for a review and Owens [1991, pp. 373–375] for a unique listing.) Included are techniques such as expansion, modeling, and contingent queries which serve to provide immediate information to the child about his discourse contributions. Table 4–6 lists some suggestions for ways to provide children with the information they might need to continue in the discourse event.

Some techniques have been designed to sabotage the event taking place to stimulate interest and motivate efforts to initiate or maintain the discourse effort. Table 4–7 lists some techniques, called sabotage procedures (Duchan & Weitzner-Lin, 1987) that can be used to promote learning.

Although local level discourse support has become a tried and true way to support children's communication, it is subject to difficulties when it fails to take into consideration the situatedness of the exchange. In the following example, the adult's local level responses and initiations are inappropriate because the respondent has failed to take into consideration that the reason the child is asking the question is that he is following an adult-imposed rule that requires him to ask permission to go to the bathroom.

Evidence of the Need for Situated Understanding

Semantic contingency:
 Child: I go bathroom?
 Adult: That is the bathroom.

Intent contingency:
 Child: I go bathroom?
 Adult: You're asking to go to the bathroom.

Expansion (recasts):
 Child: I go bathroom?
 Adult: You want to go to the bathroom?

Expansion plus:
 Child: Go bathroom?
 Adult: Go to the bathroom? Lots of children go to
   the bathroom.

Open-ended questions:
 Child: Go bathroom?
 Adult: I wonder why you want to go to the bathroom?

TABLE 4–6
Discourse Techniques for Providing the Language Learner with Local Level Support.

Semantic contingency: The content of what the supporter says is related to the semantic content of what the learner has just said (e.g., Cross, 1978).

Child:	Mommy sock?
Supporter:	I don't know.

Expansion: A kind of semantic contingency in which the supporter recasts the child's response in a more elaborate syntax (Cazden, 1965).

Child:	Mommy sock?
Supporter:	Is that Mommy's sock?

Expansion plus: The child's comment is recast and added to.

Child:	Mommy sock?
Supporter:	Is that mommy's sock? Yes, it's too big for you

Intent contingency: The content of what the supporter says is related to what the supporter takes to be the intent behind the child's utterances.

Child:	Mommy sock?
Supporter:	I don't know. Do you want to put it in Mommy's drawer?

Contingent queries: A question or comment that indicates to the learner that what was just said was confusing.

Child:	Mommy sock?
Supporter:	Do you want to know if that's your mommy's sock?

Backchanneling: The supporter acknowledges what the child has just said and provides encouragement to continue.

Child:	Mommy sock.
Supporter:	Uh hum. Mommy sock.

Verbal scaffolding: The supporter provides a model of what to say before the child has said it, offering a frame and option to imitate the model (Kirchner, 1991b).

Supporter:	That must be your mommy's sock.
Child:	Mommy sock.

Open-ended questions: The supporter asks the child to wonder, suppose, or consider options about what is going on (Educational Productions, 1987).

Supporter:	I wonder what this is?
Child:	Mommy sock.

TABLE 4–7

Discourse Techniques to Sabotage Communication and Thus Motivate the Child to Initiate or Maintain Discourse Efforts.

Techniques	Description
Communicative temptations	Create a context of need, and wait for the child to make a request (Wetherby & Prutting, 1984).
Contrived misunderstandings	Act confused, or ask about something the child just said (Gallagher & Darnton, 1978; Weiner & Ostrowski, 1979).
Contrived lack of response	Puzzled looks, silence (Duchan & Weitzner-Lin, 1987).
Probems in the event sequence	Flat tire on the way to the grocery store, hole in a shopping bag, cashier breaking a bottle (Culatta, 1994).

Another source of evidence that local level discourse techniques need to be grounded in the situation is from deictic indicators and the use of voice in carrying out the discourse technique. Some techniques are intended to be a revoicing of the original utterance issued by the child. But the adult who expands on the child's content is not, in fact, the child. This shift in person might thus be accompanied by a change in pronoun as in the examples in the previous box ("I" is shifted to "you" to handle the deictic shift when the adult voices what the child wants). To understand the basis of the shift, the child needs to understand that the participants have roles, (self and other), and that the roles are reflected in the organization of the discourse.

■ SUMMARY

This chapter has treated three types of contexts for supporting children on their way to more successful communications. The first context involved the ways the objects, people, and physical space can be arranged to support children's learning. It was argued that the "here and now" is actually an interpreted here and now, and that the palpably present must be richly interpreted to be fully understood.

The second context was that of the event. Sometimes children need to learn about an event in order to participate in it, at other times they can use an event to support new learnings. Mundane events of everyday life often offer the very best contexts in which to support children's new learning.

A third context was discourse. Discourse comes in different types, or genres. Children must learn how genres are structured to participate in them. Examples of discourse genres are conversations, event descriptions, stories, expositories, and lessons. The genres provide children with a global understanding, sometimes referred to as a macrostructure. Also important is a more local understanding of discourse, one that relates meanings of elements contained in nearby sentences. This level of understanding has been called the microstructure of the discourse and is manifest in the use of language indicating various types of discourse cohesion devices such as interclausal connectives and pronouns.

Sensemaking:
The Source for
Children's Language
Understanding and
Communicative
Competence

In 1932, Bartlett carried out his ingenious study in which he found that adults recall unusual events in stories by changing them to fit their own sense of the world. None of his British subjects could understand how to interpret the Native American story which included a description of something black coming out of a dead man's mouth. Their difficulty with the concept is shown by the various renditions of the nature of the black substance and its eventual omission from their verbal recollections (see Chapter 1, page 15). Bartlett hypothesized from his subjects' treatment of the black material that they were working hard to make sense of the story, and in so doing they created a new, coherent version by creating an interpretation that made sense within their other understandings of the world.

In Bartlett's experiment his subjects had difficulty at first conjuring up existing schemata to understand the unusual black substance. Goodman and her colleagues would describe the problem as one involving schema confirmation (Farrar & Goodman, 1992; Goodman, Duchan, & Sonnenmeier, 1994). Later some subjects arrived at the notion that the black substance might be a representation of a "soul," indicating that they had identified a schema for making sense of the incongruity and deployed it in later renditions of their story. This use of an identified schema to understand and recall events has been called "schema deployment" by Goodman.

Sensemaking involves not only identification and use of known schemas, but also the learning of new schemas, a process which has been dubbed schema formation (Goodman, Duchan, & Sonnenmeier, 1994). Schema formation can be viewed as the way children develop new schemas and remake old schemas to fit new experiences. The aim of scaffolding, although not stated explicitly, is to provide children with new information in the hope that they will represent it schematically as a complex whole made up of understandable subparts (i.e., they will make sense of it). Further, Vygotsky's notion of a child's "zone of proximal development" rests on the notion of encouraging children to change their existing understandings to make sense of new information (Vygotsky, 1978).

The process of sensemaking is also at work when people ascribe intentionality to what others say or do, when they interpret the actions and talk of others in light of the other person's overall agenda, when they assign cultural significance to what is going on, when they relate the gist or moral of a story or event, when they understand how elements of a text cohere, when they initiate and maintain topics in conversation, and when they figure out how to repair a communication breakdown based on what they see as the problem of misunderstanding.

The six contexts identified in the previous chapters of this book are among those used by the sensemaker to create an understanding of what is going on. Understandings within the social context provide a structure for construing one's own role and the roles of others. When used best the social context includes a deep understanding of roles required for the occasion and their reciprocal relations. The emotional context is created from the interpreters' experienced feelings of self-confidence as well as feelings about the currently experienced scene. In the intentional and motivational context, the sensemakers interpret why their partners are doing what they are doing on a particular occasion. Within this context interpreters come to understand and predict the sorts of things their interactants are likely to do. The physical context offers props in the perceived or imagined scene that the interpreter can use to put together a coherent view of how various aspects of the scene fit with an overall interpretation of what is going on. The event and discourse contexts provide a meaning focus from which to infer and interpret what is going on and what is being talked about.

The notion of sensemaking is crucial to understanding the the aims of intervention carried out in the situated pragmatics framework. The communicator, whose growth is being facilitated using a situated pragmatics approach, is being helped not only to communicate in appropriate ways, but also to develop a deep understanding of the situated meaningfulness of those contexts, what Geertz (1973b) has called a "thick description" of everyday happenings. A framework which takes as given a thick interpretation of discourse and enacted events leads to a call for a thick intervention approach, a thick therapy, a therapy we have been calling situated pragmatics.

■□ SENSEMAKING AND SOCIAL INTERACTION

Many of the programs designed to enhance social acceptance of children with disabilities treat social competence as a set of isolable skills. The approach can be traced to a behavioristic philosophy in which a set of behaviors are treated as separable responses, like atoms, which together build into a full behavioral domain. Haring (1992), himself a behaviorist, takes issue with this atomistic view, and argues that success in social interaction requires that the interactant understand what is going on in the social event and what motivations underlie the behavior of their social partners.

Critique of Social Skills Training Approaches

The idea that social competence and making friends can be broken into a series of discrete responses is counterproductive. Can social competence be defined merely in the scientific tradition of breaking it down atomistically into smaller and smaller sub-units, or is something lost when the whole is broken into parts? (p. 307)

The function of an event and its connection to the context are not necessarily served solely by the teaching of a specific skill to a learner (e.g., sharing a toy with a peer). The skill has to be understood in relation to the goals that a child has for her or his social behavior, the quality of support that the social behavior receives from others, and the

(continued)

power of the simple presence and responsiveness of
others in the child's natural settings to increase the
occurrence of the behavior. In other words, a more contex-
tualistic analysis considers the goals and functions of
behavior from the child's perspective, as well as the social
responses that the child receives in interaction with others,
which reinforce social behavior.

(Haring, 1992, p. 309)

As pointed out by Haring, to be effective in carrying out the social
skills taught in a skills' training program, children need to understand
what is going on as well as how others' are interpreting what is going on.
In this way they will be able to determine why and when to apply their
skills. It is not always appropriate to offer to share a toy or to request to
be included in an event. Behaviors that seem socially positive also need
to fit to partners' needs, wants, and understandings.

Even at the most mundane level of conversational exchanges children need to understand how partners' are thinking. Based on that understanding they can select the vocabulary and frames of reference that
will promote successful conversational exchanges. The elements of conversational interaction listed in Table 5-1 are listener sensitive, and require that a child be aware of their partners' point of view so she can
achieve her conversational and social goals. The process of adjusting
one's language to fit the perspective of another has been called fine tuning (Cross, 1978; Duchan, 1986; Lund & Duchan, 1993).

■□ SENSEMAKING AND AFFECT

Typically, affect is seen as icing on a layered cake. It is added somewhat
arbitrarily to the layers of language such as phonology, morphology,
syntax, and semantics and bears little integral relationship to them. A sentence or segment of discourse is seen as having its own meaning, and the
emotional content of the message or the emotional reaction to it is not
instrumental in altering its inherent semantic or discourse interpretation.

A framework that allows for a thicker interpretation of meaning —
one which goes beyond the language of the text — also allows for emotion to be part of what is being conveyed rather than a separate addition
to it. Communications from the heart permeate the words and are interpreted differently than the same words would be under more neutral circumstances. Messages intended to insult or reject or convey anger need

TABLE 5–1

Elements of Conversational "Fine Tuning" Which Require a Sensitivity to How a Conversational Partner Is Making Sense of What Is Going On.

---

1. Ways of indicating which information is new to the listener in contrast with talking about what is assumed to be known or shared:

New	Old
a. Use of article "a" (I saw a penguin at the zoo.)	Use of article "the" (The penguin was wearing a tux.)
b. Use of background phrases and adjectives (John, **my friend from first grade**, called me up)	Use of simple nouns (John called me up.)
c. Identifying setting (The Cincinnati zoo)	Presuming setting via deictic terms (**That** zoo)

2. Ways of helping partner interpret frame shifts:

   Use of discourse markers to signal how to interpret next segment of text (e.g., well = disagreement; then = shift in perspective; okay = we are about to begin something; anyway = we are about to return to our original theme; let's pretend = I am suggesting a shift to a new frame outside of the here and now reality).

3. Ways of helping the partner track the spatial, temporal, or subjective perspectives being conveyed in a segment of discourse:

   Use of deictic terms to fit with partner's perspective (e.g., spatial directions or descriptions originating with partners' place of departure or path — turn right in relation to where partner will be facing; temporal expressions require knowledge within a time frame — day before yesterday requires that partner know the time of writing or speaking).

4. Ways to use vocabulary and referring expressions to be in accord with the partners' presumed background knowledge:

   Select level of difficulty to match partner's presumed ability; select level of specificity to fit partner's knowledge needs; fill in details if judged necessary to help partner identify intended referent.

---

to be interpreted with feeling, as well as linguistically, to be fully understood.

Events, too, carry affective meaning which may have a considerable influence on a child's sense of those events. Stern (1985), in his discussion of the literature on social referencing, describes a mother who emitted nonverbal signals of depression whenever her son knocked something over (see Stern's example below).

**A Mother's Affective Treatment
of Her Son's Maladroit Behavior**

Whenever her son did something maladroit, as is expectable in a one-year-old, so that something got knocked over or a toy was disarranged, the mother would let out a multimodal depressive signal. This consisted of long expirations, falling intonations, slightly collapsing postures, furrowing the brows, tilting and drooping the head, and "Oh, Johnnys" that could be interpreted as "Look what you've done to your mother again . . . Gradually, Johnny's exuberant exploratory freedom became more circumspect. His mother too had brought an alien affective experience into an otherwise neutral or positive activity.

(Stern, 1985, p. 222)

Stern (1985) also described in detail the sincerity with which adults communicate affect. For example, adults may feign enthusiasm about a second event in order to direct infants attention away from something dangerous. Or adults may allow an exciting interaction to proceed with "one foot on the brakes," decelerating children's growing excitement when they shows signs of overload (Stern, 1985). Affect is part of the adult's sensemaking and is likely to influence how the child makes sense of what is happening. It is an important means of communication, and can be used to positive or negative ends by both partners!

■□ SENSEMAKING AND INTENTIONALITY

When an adult tells a child what to say, he or she may be putting unwanted words in a child's mouth. This is clear in contexts in which children are required to say "I'm sorry" when they don't feel apologetic, to say "thank you" when they don't feel grateful, or to repeat a sentence using the correct linguistic forms. We refer to these situations as those in which the child performs automatically or uses "rote" language. But "rote" can mean either that the child is saying something without assigning it the hoped-for intent (i.e., he isn't really sorry, he doesn't really feel thankful) or that the child doesn't understand the words (he acts like a mynah bird, just repeating what he heard). Although both meanings of "rote" are pertinent to an effort aimed at getting the child to communicate effectively, the **intent** is what will be addressed here. That is to say, we are concerned with the aspect of sensemaking that involves the child's understanding that words are useful and that one's own communications as well as those of others' are designed not only to convey a semantically coded message but also to achieve a communicative goal such as to request, apologize, or convey thanks.

Sensemaking, when tied to intent, can be viewed from the point of view of either communicative partner. When viewed from one's own perspective sensemakers construe the current situation in light of their personal goals, both immediate and long term — having fun, making friends, getting one's turn on the slide. When interacting with someone else, sensemakers need to determine others' intents to interpret the motivation behind their verbal or nonverbal behavior.

There is a gray area of overlap area between one's own and another's intent present in many communicative situations — especially those involving some type of language modeling or teaching. Imagine a teacher who asks a child to say "I want a cookie" before the child is issued the cookie. The teacher's intent in this case is to get the child to ask for something that the teacher presumes the child wants. When the child imitates the teacher's sentence, does she understand that that sentence is an expression of her own intent rather than that of the teacher? What if, instead, the child comes to understand the sentence is something that the teacher requires to be done before she gives something away — like saying "please." Or perhaps the child sees the verbal request as part of a ritual, thus failing to understand how the words are meaningfully related to her own intent. Even for the child who understands the words, do they convey the same intent in this context of imitation that they would if spontaneously produced? We know from experience, for example, that when someone mocks another, the intent or agenda conveyed in the original is not usually part of the imitation.

This issue of authenticity of intents is not particular to contexts in which teachers tell students what to say. It is a common occurrence and has been studied under the category of voice. Bakhtin (1981) suggested that a particular utterance, although issued by an individual, has in it traces of other voices from the surrounding discourse. An answer to a question contains the voice of the questioner. Not until the author assumes authority over the utterance by adding his intent and accent, does it take on the signature of that individual. (See the following box and Chapter 1 for more on the voice of Bakhtin.)

How An Utterance Can Have More Than One Voice

The work in language is half someone else's. It becomes "one's own" only when the speaker populates it with his own intention, his own accent, when he appropriates the word, adapting it to his own semantic and expressive intention. Prior to this moment of appropriation, the word does not exist in a neutral and impersonal language (it is not, after all, out of a dictionary that the speaker gets his words!), but rather it exists in other people's mouths, in other people's contexts, serving other people's intentions; it is from there that one must take the word, and make it one's own.

(Bakhtin, 1981, pp. 293–294)

◼️ SENSEMAKING IN A PHYSICAL CONTEXT

A common way of rendering children's learning is that they progress from being focused on the impinging physical context to a stage where they can think and talk about matters distanced from the current situation (Norris & Hoffman, 1993a; Werner & Kaplan, 1963). Children at the one- or two-word stage of language development, whether typical or atypical learners, have been assumed by many to be naming the objects, actions, or events that are taking place before them (e.g., "Mommy sock" Rough translation: This sock that I am now looking at is mommy's sock). Later, these children will able to talk about abstract ideas, unrelated to what they are seeing or hearing (e.g.,"No lion hurt?" Rough translation: Since we're talking about our impending trip to the zoo, I wonder if I need to be worried about the lions hurting me).

A situated view of children's first communications does not see the child's effort as one of naming objects physically present, but rather as part of a complex involving social interaction; one accompanied by affect, intents, events, and related to the preceding and anticipated discourse. The child who said "Mommy sock" may have wanted to get the attention of his mother to let her know that he recognized the sock as hers. The child could have uttered this as he remembered the game he and his mother played a few days earlier when she was sorting the clothes and identifying the individual items for her child. His sensemaking is much richer than would be depicted under a view that portrays him as simply associating the object he sees with its name.

Given the situated view of first language learning, what then is the status of the theory that says children at this stage are fixated on the physical here and now? Although answers to this question from the research literature are only suggestive, theorizing would suggest that children's early sensemaking involves memories and abstractions that build on the here and now. What differentiates early from later learning is that children's first words are anchored in the physical context, whereas at later stages children are better able to anchor their thoughts and communications in a mental experience as well as a physical experience.

■□ MAKING SENSE OF EVENTS

Schema theory sometimes renders events as sequences of actions holding logical or temporal relations with one another. Scripts have been described as events which are frequently occurring, carried out by people with assigned role relations, with similar props, and activities. What is absent from this depiction of events are the deeper meanings that some events might have for their participants. Weddings, birthday parties, and even mealtimes are likely to mean more to those engaged in them than is portrayed by the skeletal view of structured relations. When the more elaborate, meaningful understanding of events is missing, it results in what children call "not getting it." It is what people who don't understand football feel when watching a game, or what those who are outside a religion or culture feel when participating in a ceremony they don't understand.

Why Some Children "Don't Get It"

To the extent that children have sufficient language skill to process the spoken and written language of education and to connect it to the nonverbal context and prior knowledge, they are able to do what children call "getting it," by comprehending and participating in the broadest sense in their own learning. To the extent that children have inadequate language skills and related strategies for making sense of the world of school, they often "don't get it."

(Nelson, 1989, pp. 170–171)

■□ SENSEMAKING AND DISCOURSE

Children and adults who are engaged in the enterprise of making sense of what is going on around them do so by using not only the text but whatever they take to be pertinent for current understanding. This view of the centrality of sensemaking for understanding events as well as the language within them is at variance with the view that texts can be interpreted on their own. The sensemaking view has been called the "open view" of text interpretation, where meanings that are outside the confines of the text can be provided. A less useful "closed view," on the other hand, is one in which texts are seen as self-contained, with the meanings found within the boundaries of the text.

Halliday and Hasan's (1976) work on discourse cohesion is an example of the more constrained and less useful "closed text" view. In their now-classic book, *Cohesion in English*, they identified a set of linguistic devices which function to tie components of a text together. These elements in a text, such as words, clauses, or sentences, are portrayed as isolable units; and the cohesion devices are depicted as functioning to connect these elements. The result is the creation of textual cohesion. Examples of cohesion devices identified by Halliday and Hasan are interclausal conjunctions (e.g., and, but, then), rementions of the same word (lexical reiteration), pronominal referencing (endophoric ties), and rementions of a particular referent with using different referring expressions (lexical substitution).

An alternative approach to Halliday and Hasan is the open text view forwarded by Deborah Schiffrin and others (Duchan, Bruder, & Hewitt, in press; Lund & Duchan, 1993; Schiffrin, 1987; Segal, Duchan, & Scott, 1991). In this open view, the work of cohesion takes place in the minds of those interpreting the text. The interpretation includes much more than the meanings of the words and sentences. The interpreter's job in an open view of text interpretation is to conjure up a mental model of what is going on. The model includes imputed relations of people, places, events, and background information about them. Two elements such as "sugar" and "flour," which do not contribute to cohesion in Halliday and Hasan's conceptual framework, can be related in the open text view by virtue of being conceptualized as ingredients in a particular recipe. Further, the open text view allows for devices to signal disconnectedness or noncohesion. For example, rather than seeing "then" as an indicator of temporal relatedness between clauses, the open text view has rendered it as a marker of discourse disjuncture separating conceptual understandings of discourse from one another (Duchan, Meth, & Waltzman, 1992; Schiffrin, 1987; Segal, Duchan, & Scott, 1991). Duchan et al. (1992) found that "then" was used by adults describing a film to mark shifts in the place being filmed or in the point of view of an invisible cameraman.

◼️ FRAMING AS A TYPE OF SENSEMAKING

Besides the six contexts focused on in this book, there is a seventh context that is central to the process of sensemaking, and within which all sensemaking takes place — **framing**. A particular communicative act can be interpreted in multiple ways, some of which will depend on a frame of reference within which the act is regarded. A raised fist means something when it occurs in a demonstration, in play, or in a fight. Teaching, pretending, and common reality provide context frames within which happenings are understood. Further, different frames allow different things to happen. In the worlds of pretense and fiction, mice can talk, superhumans can fly, and time can shift to the future (Segal, in press). Erving Goffman (1974) in his exegesis of frames of reality analyzed how bracketed realities, such as those involved in demonstrations and dramas, are indicated and interpreted in light of a primary reality, that of everyday experiences.

Children use reality frames in their early play, as evidenced by their use of terms such as "let's pretend," to mark frame shifts from the play to the "real world" exchange. Smilanski and Sheftaya (1990) when analyzing the language used by Israeli kindergartners concluded that the sentences beginning with "let's pretend" are one player's solicitations of permission from his playmates to introduce a new idea or object into their pretend world. The following statements are solicitations by Smilanski and Sheftaya's kindergarten subjects to introduce something from the real world into the pretend world.

**Examples of Use of "Let's Pretend"
by Kindergarten Children to Mark a Shifting
Out and Back to the Play Frame**

(Numbers refer to order of utterances in the transcript)

2. Ruth: Let's pretend both have the measles.

6. Ruth: (after a brief exchange about who owns the doctor's bag)
You know, she is sick, she has the measles.

(continued)

> 7. Tamar: If she has the measles, she shouldn't have cough syrup.
>
> 3. Sarah: Let's pretend it was a blood test.
>
> 24. Ruth: A blood test is taken from the finger!
>
> 25. Tamar: I did it from the foot.
>
> 36. Ruth: Let's pretend you are a dog.
>
> 37. David: Good, then you feed me.
>
> 47. David: Let's pretend that this is my bone.
>
> 48. Ruth: Now come dear puppy, let's go home.
>
> 50. Tamar: Let's pretend we are closing the clinic. Now I'm not the doctor anymore.
>
> 51. Tamar: I will be your baby (to Sarah)
>
> 52. Sarah: No you are my big girl in the Army.
>
> 56. David: Let's pretend that dogs like chewing gum.
>
> 57. Ruth: No, only candy. (Offers David imaginary candy.)
>
> (Smilanshi & Sheftaya, 1990, pp. 4–6)

An important issue in language intervention is whether things experienced within the teaching frame are translated into other frames, especially into the frame of primary reality (Nietupski, Hamre-Nietupski, Clancy, & Verrhusen, 1986). Will children who practice an everyday simulation activity in the classroom see the relationship between that activity and the intended target event? Do children who practice going to a grocery store in the classroom understand how that event works in the community? Framing thus becomes tied to the issue of generalization, and offers another way of thinking about successes or blocks to achieving "carryover."

A second issue that framing raises for language interventionists is whether metalanguage or "language about language" creates a frame shift that makes language learning more difficult. Our responses of "good talking" or "say your sound in that word" can be considered a frame shift in that the move is out of the frame of direct communication and into the frame of analyzing communication.

◼️ SENSEMAKING AS A WAY TO PROVIDE COMMUNICATIVE SUPPORT

Planning intervention with the child's sensemaking in mind would lead to a number of guiding principles that could help along the way (see

TABLE 5-2
Some Guiding Principles for Bringing Sensemaking into Language Intervention.

1. The **goals** of language intervention programs should be prioritized and those that have the greatest impact on the child's improved sensemaking should be given the highest priority.

2. When determining the intervention **activities**, choose those that make sense in the child's life and are sensible in the child's cultural context.

3. If there is a need to break down language, events, or discourse into component parts to facilitate learning, **divide the tasks** in ways that are meaningful for the child.

4. When asking **questions** to promote understandings, ask authentic questions — ones you would like to know the answers to.

5. Use **physical props** that are meaningful to the child.

6. **Respond contingently** to the child's intent, content, and form, giving priority to the intent.

7. Minimize **frame shifts** caused by correction or metalinguistic rewards (e.g., "Remember how you're supposed to say that?" "Good talking").

8. Follow the children's lead. Talk with them about what they may be thinking.

9. Consider the **function** as well as form as part of a child's response, and respond accordingly. (Avoid focusing soley on "right answers.")

Duchan, 1986 for a more detail treatment of this topic). Table 5-2 presents a few.

■ SUMMARY

Sensemaking is at the center of what context support is intended to achieve. Providing children with support is only successful if they can make sense of that support in relation to what they are learning. Working within a child's conceptual grasp (what Vygotsky, 1978, has called zone of proximal development) provides the child with meaningful support for learning (cues, information, input, hints, discourse structure). What is crucial is the support that make sense to the child in light of what he or she knows and is experiencing in the current situation —a situated pragmatics kind of sense.

The Influence
of Culture
on Children's
Language Learning

Malinowski (1922) was among the first to see the job of an anthropologist as one of discovering the influences of culture on the behaviors its members. Since that time, a group of sociolinguists have developed a subspecialty sometimes called the "ethnography of communication" (Hymes, 1972) wherein communication is studied cross-culturally. The result has been that cultures have been found to differ in how they regard communication (Bauman & Sherzer, 1989; Sherzer, 1983), in their evaluation of children's language learning (Schieffelin & Ochs, 1986), in who is assigned the role of socializing children (Crago & Eriks-Brophy, 1994; Schieffelin, 1994), in how stories are organized (Heath, 1983; Michaels, 1981), and in the functions and organization of communicative events (Schieffelin, 1990; Watson-Gegeo & Gegeo, 1986).

Following in the tradition of ethnographers of communication, one can (and must) extend the notion of situated pragmatics to include the ways children's home culture influences their communication. The success a child will have in adjusting to the schools of a new culture will be importantly affected by the fit between the experiences provided in his or her home culture and those of their new school (Heath, 1983, 1986; Michaels, 1981, 1986). Clinical intervention approaches need to be tailored to fit the cultural practices of the children being supported (van Kleek, 1994).

The cultural bias in our existing approaches has been pointed out by van Kleek (1994) in her description of the assumptions underlying parent training approaches commonly used which aim to help parents encourage and respond in specific ways to their child's communications. Table 6–1 shows that many cultural assumptions made by such programs may not be valid for children who come from cultures other than mainstream, middle-class, Anglo-American.

The six ways of viewing situatedness that have been developed in previous chapters can provide a frame of reference for viewing the role of culture on children's learning to communicate. Researchers of culture offer us an interesting set of discoveries in each of the six domains. Their findings can be used to guide our efforts as we develop supportive learning contexts to fit children's cultural understandings.

Culture and Social Context

The social contexts that children grow up in will depend on the roles they are assigned as children. Some cultures foster independence in children, bending rules and ways of doing things to fit children's wants and needs. Other cultures aim to have their children understand conformance to situational dictates, regardless of the personal goals. Heath, for example, describes how Chinese-Americans emphasize situational goals over those of the individual.

Roles of Children in the Chinese-American Culture

Children are expected . . . to assume responsibilities according to their age and sex. Moreover, they are expected to play roles and perform duties independently of their personal feelings or goals. Parents see themselves as primary agents in directing children to assume in appropriate fashion the roles that the community expects of boys and girls . . . Children must defer to adults, who determine what their children can do and tell them when they should do it . . . . Learning is centered on the situation rather than

---

> the individual, because the individual must center on the situation in order to adjust to both the familiar environment and new circumstances.
>
> (Heath, 1986, p. 158)

The **social roles** children assume are reflected in the communication patterns of the culture. Cultures vary in who talks to whom and the nature of that talk. The culture thereby determines the pragmatics of the members' communications and specifies the social contexts in which children come to understand what roles to take. The following examples show how the communicative roles of children vary across cultures.

TABLE 6-1
Assumptions Made by Many Parent Training Programs That May Not Be Culturally Appropriate for Many Children or Their Families.

1. By focusing on parents it is assumed that parents are the child's primary caregiver.

2. By targeting parent-child interaction, it is assumed that the predominant pattern of interaction in the family is two-party or dyadic.

3. By attempting to increase the child's overall amount of verbal interaction, it is assumed that the family values children talking a lot.

4. By working to get the child to initiate more communication, it is assumed that the family believes children should initiate conversation with adults.

5. By asking the adult to communicate at the child's level, it is assumed that the family believes adults should make accommodations to young children.

6. By asking adults to provide words or sentences that they think the child is intending . . . . it is assumed that the family believes one can know another's intentions.

7. By advocating a conversational style to promote language development, it is assumed that the family believes that children learn language best as equal participants in conversation.

Source: From van Kleeck, A. (1994). Potential cultural bias in training parents as conversational partners with their children who have delays in language development, pp. 67–68. *American Journal of Spech-Language Pathology, 3,* 67–78, with permission.

Cultural Variations When Assigning Communicative Roles

The Inuit of Northern Alaska:

In general, children talk to children. Older siblings have communicative interactions with young children that include teasing and repetition routines. Adults talk with adults, sometimes at length and sometimes with great economy of speech. Adults have communicative interactions with young children that include directives, affectionate talk, teasing ignoring their children's intrusions and questions, and companionable and disciplinary silence. Children talk with adults but not usually by asking questions nor when adults are conversing.

(Crago & Eriks-Brophy, 1994, p. 48)

Chinese-Americans:

In conversational exchanges, parents control topics, length of time for talk by children, and the direction of conversation. Parents initiate conversation with children, ask them factual questions, talk about steps they are following as they go about tasks, and monitor their children's talk and activities through verbal correction, explication, and evaluation.

(Heath, 1986, p. 158)

Culture and Affect

Cultures vary in the ways they teach children to feel and in their expressions of those feelings. The children in Samoa are taught to request things by portraying themselves as feeling needy (Ochs, 1988). These children learn to cast their requests as self-deprecations or what Ochs calls "begging" by using a term "poor me" along with their request. Ochs observes that when young Samoan children make requests using these self-effacing structures, they are more successful in getting what they want.

Ochs also has described verbal expressions used by Samoan adults to conveying affection to children. She shows that the adults use these expressions to evoke in the children feelings of sympathy toward others. For example, an adult will say "Don't bother your dear little sibling" to persuade the child to change his behavior toward a sibling. On other occasions of a child's wrongdoing, a caregiver might warn or threaten the child to engender fear and thereby get the child to stop (Ochs, 1988). Finally, if a child is thought to have lied or refuses to do what is required, an adult might respond by "shaming" or "challenging" the child, calling him or her "prideful, bossy," or "acting like a European" (not wanting to do dirty work). Or the adult may challenge the veracity of a child's statement by asking another child to affirm or deny it.

Goodwin (1990) has shown the role affect plays in the verbal disputes of African-American girls in Philadelphia, Pennsylvania. She found the girls, ranging in age from 4 to 13 years, engaged in what they called "instigations." Instigations involved a child finding out that others had talked about her behind her back and later confronting the others about the violation of her dignity. Goodwin (1990) describes these acts of violation and confrontations as passionate, and summarizes their function in the friends' culture as ways the girls "can call forth feelings of righteous indignation that are relevant to the shaping of a dispute which can last for over a month" (p. 286).

Cultures also vary in what they take to be contexts of embarrassment and ways to save oneself from embarrassment. Goffman's notion of face saving has provided researchers of culture with a way of describing these cultural differences. For example, in their ethnographic research on the Inuit teacher-student interactions in classrooms of Northern Quebec, Crago and Eriks-Brophy have observed a variety of ways teachers avoid embarrassing their children during teaching interactions (Crago & Eriks-Brophy, 1994; Eriks-Brophy & Crago, 1993). The teachers tended to direct their questions toward the class as a group, rather than to individual children. Calling on individual children was regarded by the Inuit teachers as "forcing" students to participate and as resulting in making the students "feel bad."

Nor did the Inuit teachers publicly evaluate the responses of individual children. Rather, they would interact with students who were not responding conventionally in private, providing feedback on an individual basis. The teachers also had the students interact in small groups to complete assigned tasks, thereby fostering peer support rather than taking directions from an authoritarian teacher.

An Example of an Inuit Teacher's Efforts to Avoid Embarrassing a Student Who Was Not Responding Correctly

Six students and the teacher were seated in a semi-circle on the floor. The teacher modeled with one student's

(continued)

> materials how she wanted the activity to be set up, making only occasional comments. One student was having difficulty arranging the appropriate units and number cards to form the desired numeral. The teacher repeated the directives often . . . subtly directing the group to look for errors in their work. She called the student's name softly once but made no other comment. Finally she moved over to the student and tapped lightly on the number seven card, showing the student his error without speaking. The student then fixed the error in silence. Other students did not comment on these individual corrections.
> (Crago & Eriks-Brophy, 1994, p. 15)

Like the Inuit, the Hawaiian natives from the Warm Springs Reserve also have a deep commitment for saving face. The members of this culture avoid calling undue attention to individuals in conversation, avoid situations involving social control, and avoid putting themselves above others in social interactions (Philips, 1983).

Culture and Intentionality

The creation and interpretation of single speech acts are heavily influenced by one's culture. Even within a culture, there may be differences between how individual speech acts intents are generated, expressed, and interpreted. Tannen (1990), in her oft-quoted book on gender differences in carrying out conversations, makes a convincing case that males and females in mainstream American cultures are motivated to achieve different goals from their conversations. She shows from her examples of miscommunications that females, when they offer a choice or request information, are attempting to achieve social goals related to developing intimacy such as making a friendly suggestion or trying to meet someone. A male, with a different cultural perspective, interprets choice questions and requests for information as compromising his goal of achieving independence. Within that view he interprets her overtures as a sign of indecisiveness or being uninformed. Some males' reticence to ask directions is attributed by Tannen to their unwillingness to expose their ignorance, as in the example on the next page.

Although Tannen's example focuses on particular intents behind a specific speech act, requesting directions, the discrepancy in the male and female interpretations has to do with a larger issue, the **agendas** of

---

Male and Female Difference in Issuing and Interpreting Single-act Speech Acts

Sitting in the front seat of the car beside Harold, Sybil is fuming. They have been driving around for half an hour looking for a street he is sure is close by. Sybil is angry not because Harold does not know the way, but because he insists on trying to find it himself rather than stopping and asking someone. Her anger stems from viewing his behavior through the lens of her own: If she were driving, she would have asked directions as soon as she realized she didn't know which way to go, and they'd now be comfortably ensconced in their friends' living room instead of driving in circles, as the hour gets later and later. Since asking directions does not make Sybil uncomfortable, refusing to ask makes no sense to her. But in Harold's world, driving around until he finds his way is the reasonable thing to do, since asking for help makes him uncomfortable. He's avoiding that discomfort and trying to maintain his sense of himself as a self-sufficient person.

(Tannen, 1990, p. 62)

---

the participants. Ethnographers, while not using the rubric of agenda, have revealed a number of different agendas which reflect the mores of the cultures they study. For example, some have studied ways speakers accomplish their culturally promoted agendas such as those involved in teasing, threatening, challenging, clarifying, or counseling and have found the tactics and discourse styles to vary across cultures (Crago, 1988; Miller, 1986; Ochs, 1988; Schieffelin, 1990; Sherzer, 1983).

Cultural Influences from the Physical Context

Children's physical environment will depend on where they live and who they live with. Some cultures provide children with toys to play with, with children's books to read. Others do not. In some cultures children have their own possessions; in others objects, toys, and clothes are communally owned. Cultures and neighborhoods will differ in the places available to children for play and exploration. All these sources of variability yield different life experiences, different ways of thinking, and different ways of communicating for children of different cultural groups.

In the following box Ward describes how physical surroundings can affect children's life experiences.

The Physical Life Context of African-American Children Living in a Community in the Rural South

In addition to the yard in which every child plays, there are sugar cane fields adjoining the lots. Before the fall harvest, the sweet round sticks are an endless source of amusement. The other fields either lie fallow or provide pasture for the cattle. The paths across the fields, the junk thrown in them, and the pecan groves are playgrounds for all children. No yards are fenced and all contain open sewers in which to play. The lack of sidewalks, closed sewers, curbs, paved roads, or inside storage facilities creates a feeling of dirt and clutter. However, the yard with its clothespins, bottles, pigpen, various tubs and cans, old cars, sticks, tools, automobile parts, and running sewer water, is a child's richest playground.

(Ward, 1971, p. 37)

Events of Different Cultures

Those who have studied the ways adults help children learn about their world have found striking cross-cultural differences. Some cultures do not engage in direct teaching, but rather wait for children to learn on their own (Heath, 1983). In other cultures, there is direct teaching, in which children are taught "how to be" in the various everyday events. For example, Schieffelin (1990), Crago and Eriks-Brophy (1994), and Heath (1986) have all reported cultural contexts in which adults and older children of the culture presented young children with a variety of verbal routines, and told the children what to say for those different occasions. The caregivers indicated the intended phrase with the term meaning "say (do) it this way" (see examples on the next page).

Along with these important mundane activities, which are taken for granted by members of the culture, are events that are highlighted and emphasized by cultures — the events that occur on celebrated holidays. Lynch and Hanson (1992), in their guide to professionals for how to develop cross-cultural competence, list significant cultural events for Native Americans as well as for North Americans with ethnic origins in

Teaching Routines Used by Different Cultural Groups

Kaluli, from Papua New Guinea:

Caregivers use **elema** with young children to perform a variety of functions in discourse and interactions. Depending on the situation and the participants involved, **elema** can occur with high frequency within a given speech event. **Elema** is a verbal form of social assistance that provides children with specific lines tailored to specific addressees. Children are thus able to enter into interactions as active participants and accomplish with support what they may not yet be able to do alone. **Elema** routines are important because they provide not only the content of talk but the form and the function as well. They are not staged or done simply for practice, but are embedded in ongoing interaction. What young children say in **elema** routines has real consequences for the shape and outcome of an event.

(Schieffelin, 1990, p. 77)

Inuit, from Northern Quebec:

Young Inuit children are also encouraged to model verbal behavior on that of their older siblings through repetition or imitation routines. In these routines, the children are instructed to say something by being told to repeat after their caregivers. For verbal material, Inuit instruct their children to model or repeat by saying **lalaurit** (say it like this). Verbal repetition routines used with four Inuit children we studied were primarily used by young mothers, teen-aged caregivers, or siblings. They were of two main types: routines that often took place in triadic settings in which the child was instructed on how to greet and acknowledge greetings, and repetition routines used to get young children to say phrases in English, including politeness conventions and counting.

(Crago & Eriks-Brophy, 1994, p. 46)

Mainstream School-Oriented Activities in the United States:

Label quests . . . are language activities in which adults either name items or ask for their names. With very young

(continued)

children, adults name the item, usually pointing to it or holding it in front of the child. As children learn to say words, adults ask "What's this?" "Who's that?" Label quests include not only the names of items, but their attributes as well ...

Throughout school, but particularly in the primary grades, teachers ask students to give them the names and attributes of items used in the classroom, read about in books, and discussed in class. Textbooks rank questions that ask "what" and "what kind of" as their easiest.

(Heath, 1986, p. 168)

in Africa, Latin America, the Philippines, different Asian countries, the Pacific Islands, the Mideast, and Europe. Nostalgic views of culture often foreground the significance of events such as these.

But it is not just going to the event that provides the cultural members with significant memories. Geertz (1973a), in his analysis of a Balinese cockfight, argued that events accrue significance that is deeper than merely being a social and ritualized occasion. The significance comes from how the event ties to the cultural meanings that go beyond the surface depiction of who was there and what they did (see the following example). Geertz calls the deep interpretations of significant events a "thick description" and argues that anything less fails to capture the true importance of cultural celebrations.

A Thick Interpretation of a Balinese Ceremony

In the cockfight, man and beast, good and evil, ego and id, the creative power of aroused masculinity and the destructive power of loosened animality fuse in a bloody drama of hatred, cruelty, violence, and death. It is little wonder that when, as is the invariable rule, the owner of the winning cock takes the carcass of the loser — often torn limb from limb by its enraged owner — home to eat, he does so with a mixture of social embarrassment, moral satisfaction, aesthetic disgust, and cannibal joy. Or that a man who has lost an important fight is sometimes driven to wreck his family shrines and curse the gods, an act of metaphysical (and social) suicide. Or that in seeking earthy analogues

> for heaven and hell the Balinese compare the former to the
> mode of a man whose cock has just won, the latter to that
> of a man whose cock has just lost.
>
> (Geertz, 1973a, pp. 420–421)

A comparable "thick description" is found in the following box, a
depiction of the cultural significance of the boxing match for fans in the
United States.

**Joyce Carol Oates' (1987) on the Significance
of Boxing for Aficionados in the United States
and a Thick Description of the Difference Between
Boxing as Skill vs. Boxing as Fighting**

Though boxing has long been popular in many countries
and under many forms of government, dictatorships no
less than democracies, surely its popularity in the States
since the days of John L. Sullivan has a good deal to do
with what Americans honor as the spirit of the individual — his "physical" spirit — in defiance of the State.
(p. 114)

It should be understood that "boxing" and "fighting," though always combined in the greatest of boxers can
be entirely different and even unrelated activities. Ama-
teur boxers are trained to win their matches on points;
professionals usually try for knockouts . . . If boxing is frequently, in the lighter weights especially, a highly complex
and refined skill, belonging solely to civilization, fighting
belongs to something predating civilization, the instinct
not merely to defend oneself — for how has the masculine
ego ever been assuaged by so minimal a response to threat?
— but to attack another and to force him into absolute sub-
mission. This accounts for the electrifying effect upon a
typical fight crowd when fighting suddenly emerges out of
boxing — when, for instance, a boxer's face begins to
bleed and the fight seems to enter a new and more dangerous phase. The flash of red is the visible sign of the fight's

(continued)

> authenticity in the eyes of many spectators and boxers are justified in being proud, as many are, of their facial scars. (pp. 49–50)

Discourse and Cultural Variability

One important aspect of acculturation for children is to learn the discourse genres of their cultural group (Heath, 1986). Cultures have been found to differ not only in the genres they emphasize or use, but also in the ways a particular genre is carried out (Smith, 1987; Tannen, 1980). For example, Hinds (1983) has reported that there is an expository writing schema in Japanese that does not exist in English. Smith (1987) has described Japanese apologies as functioning not only an admission of fault but also, unlike in America, functioning as a "social lubricant, where both parties in any interaction accept mutual responsibility" for what happened (Smith, 1987, pp. 1–2).

Differences in the use of genres by members of different cultures have been studied by Heath (1982). She identified four types of discourse genres which were differentially used by members of three nearby cultural groups in the United States' South. The first genre Heath calls **recounts**. They are event descriptions that are retold by a "teller" and are already known to the listener. Recounts may be fictional or real and occur in contexts in which one person asks another to retell something for the benefit of a third party. They thus have the quality of a performance. In other cultures, adults rarely encourage children to recount events. For example, children's recounts are seldom elicited by recently immigrated Mexican-American adults (within the past two decades) nor by Chinese-American adults (Heath, 1986). However, this discourse genre is common among Anglo-American middle class parents and school teachers in North American classrooms.

A second of Heath's discourse types she calls **accounts**. Accounts are also event descriptions, but, unlike recounts, the teller is likely to initiate the telling on his or her own rather than via a request by another person. Accounts also are new to the listener and thereby function to provide new information rather than as a performance or a test of knowledge about known information. Unlike recounts, accounts occur frequently in Mexican-American as well as Chinese-American families, and are often carried out by children in those homes (Heath, 1986). Accounts in both cultures may be evaluated for their plausibility or for whether the behavior described by the children was appropriate. Mexican-American

adults may add moral summations to the accounts of children to enhance their learning or for the benefit of younger children who are lis-
tening in. Accounts are rare in the general stream of events in schools,
except in contexts of show and tell or creating writing.

Eventcasts are a type of discourse in which events are described as
they are happening or being anticipated. Adults engage in eventcasts when
they are explicating a future event or trying to solve a problem. Children
in some cultures may create eventcasts as they are carrying out their play
or as they plan play with their friends. Eventcasts are common in the discourse of adults and children in Chinese-American families (Heath,
1986). In Mexican-American families daily events are seldom discussed
with children. However, family members may create eventcasts together
when planning future events. Teachers in mainstream American classrooms often use eventcasts as a mode of instruction when telling children
what they should do or how a schedule will be enacted (Heath, 1986).

Although the first three of Heath's discourse categories involve
event descriptions, the fourth departs from that genre. **Stories**, she sees
as fictional accounts. Usual depictions of stories, not discussed in Heath,
are that they are built around a plot in which characters get in and then
out of trouble (see, for example, Stein & Glenn, 1979). Chinese-American families engage in storytelling during book-reading events; Mexi-
can-Americans frequently tell one another stories and young children
enact stories during dramatic play. In typical American schools stories
are used as a supplement to factual learning. They are found in basal
readers, history texts, and literary materials. Teachers may have children
write or tell stories to enhance a language arts program or to enliven
moral or thematic learnings.

Three Examples of the Discourse Genres

The first is an adult using the genre (AU), the second is an
adult eliciting the genre (AE) the third is the child using
the genre (CU), and fourth the child eliciting the genre (CE).

Recount (two members know what happened, one asks for
a recount)

> AU: Remember when we saw the elephant at the zoo?
> He wasn't very friendly, was he?

> AE: Tell daddy what happened at the zoo.

(continued)

CU: Mommy and I saw an elephant spit at some people.

CE: Mom, let's tell dad what the elephant did.

Account (participants do not know what happened)

AU: Mom's car broke down and she's at the garage waiting for it to be fixed.

AE: What happened in school today?

CU: Tom's got a new bike for his birthday. It's a two wheeler.

CE: Where's mom?

Eventcast (a running commentary of current or future activities)

AU: Here the boy is riding his bike. He hit a rock, and look at this, he fell down and hurt his knee.

AE: What's happening here?

CU: The boy is crying. He hurt his knee.

CE: What's she doing now? What's in there?

Story (a narrative in which plans are thwarted, and solutions arrived at)

AU: And he couldn't find his way home. So his father went to find him, and there he was, sitting under the tree.

AE: Tell me a story about this picture?

CU: The boy was lost, and his dad discovered him at last.

CE: Read me this book?

Also relevant for cultural understandings of discourse are the ways cultures define a particular genre. For example, event accounts and stories have been found to vary considerably from one cultural group to another (Heath, 1983; Michaels, 1986; Michaels & Cazden, 1986).

Michaels (1986) found cultural variation in children's classroom presentations of event descriptions. One child, from an African-American community, used parallel structuring in her presentation of an account of her weekend activities. She described different episodes separately and then drew them together at the end. She signaled the boundaries between the episodes with intonation and stress markings. Other children gave single episode accounts in keeping with the teacher's effort to have the children talk about one thing at a time. Michaels concluded that the event, a sharing time in the classroom, unknowingly favored one type of accounting over another, thereby exhibiting cultural bias.

Heath also found consistent cultural variability in the discourse of members of different communities. The stories of one community required that the tellers keep to the facts and provide a moral. A second community told stories which elaborated on the truth, telling stories where the protagonists powers are exaggerated. Their stories needed no moral but were judged on their entertainment value rather than their lesson (Heath, 1983). Heath compared the story genres of these two communities with those favored by the school culture, and ventures an explanation of children's school success based on the similarities between home and school discourse genres.

Creating Language Learning Contexts That Are Sensitive to Culture

Cultural sensitivity in language teaching has just begun to be addressed by clinicians, teachers, and researchers. One effort has been to examine the school's culture and determine what children from other cultures need to know to succeed in school. For example, Heath has applied her ethnographic approach to discover crucial ways in which cultures vary and may differ from the school culture (see Table 6-2 for a listing). Language intervention would need to involve an assessment of the situational contexts at home and school, and a determination of how they differ in ways such as those outlined by Heath (1982). The effort of the intervention would be to bridge the gap between the two so that children and teachers may more easily develop bicultural understandings required for school success.

When the home and school are found to differ in the ways such as those outlined in Table 6-2, the options open to those supporting the children's learning are several. First, the supporter might focus on the home context and work with families **to change home contexts to be more in keeping with those of the school**. This approach was taken by Heath and Banscombe (1986), in conjunction with Thomas, a parent of a child whose culture differed from that of the school. Thomas' culture was not one in which children were read to, and children from her community had difficulty in achieving success in school. Although parenting in Thomas' culture did not entail book reading, she agreed to create a

TABLE 6–2
Discourse Contexts Affecting Children's Ability to Transition from Home to School Culture.

1. Do members of the home culture read books with their children?

2. What is the nature of the interaction during book reading at home and school? Are the children read to? Does book reading involve discussion? Does it involve examining elements of the pictures?

3. Are children asked test questions at home? At school? (Test questions are like recounts in which the questioner knows the answer and evaluates the correctness of the response.)

4. Do questions to the children focus on "what" aspects of an event? (What aspects have an analytical emphasis, where child is asked to abstract elements from a picture — What is this? What is the boy doing? What do you think will happen next?)

5. Are there questions which focus on reason? On affect? (e.g., What's that like? How must he feel?)

6. What is emphasized when reading books? Pictures? Plot? Emotion? Moral?

7. Are there discussions or questions about how parts of the book relate to one another? (gist questions, questions about the moral of stories, questions which highlight subparts of the stories — beginnings, middles, ends)

8. Is there any discussion of how stories relate to children's lives?

9. Is there a preference for factual stories? For fictional stories?

10. Who are the storytellers in the culture? Experts? Elders? Children?

11. What sort of emotion is expressed by the narrator? Are stories scary? Logical? Funny? Told for their emotional impact?

12. How does written language function in the home and school culture? To inform? For conveying instructions? To entertain?

13. How do stories function in the culture? Morality lessons? Ceremonial occasions? Competitive oratory? Entertainment?

14. When are stories told or books read to children? At bedtime? On special occasions? By special people?

Source: Adapted from Heath, S. (1982). What no bedtime story means: Narrative skills at home and at school. *Language in Society, 11,* 49–76.

book-reading bedtime event so that her preschooler could be encul-
turated into the ways of the school. Thomas provided her child with formats such as recounts, accounts, eventcasts, and stories during the course
of their interactions in a book-reading event.

A second way to bridge the home-school cultural gap is **to change
what goes on in schools to be more sensitive to the home culture**. For
example, Michaels has described her discussions with a classroom teacher about the discourse genres used by children from African-American
homes. The teacher, who had evaluated these children's oral contributions as deficient, changed her evaluation to become positive and to provide the children support for what she now saw as the children's discourse talents rather than deficits (Michaels, 1986).

Finally, Eriks-Brophy and Crago (1993) have offered a third approach which is **to design approaches that best promote children's learning, whatever their culture, and incorporate them into contexts where
they do not already exist**. Their aim is to provide positive contexts for
supporting children's learning. They take as their model the Inuit way of
interacting and suggest that it be considered for incorporation in all
classrooms, whether or not they have Inuit children in them. The approach is recommended because the Inuit do not engage in testing
children for what they know but rather work with children in an effort to
get them to collaborate with one another.

Culturally sensitive intervention which is based on situated contexts departs from other approaches which focus on teaching language
structure or overt teaching about cultural variations in dress, work, or
holidays. Intervention programs following the six themes of situated
pragmatics would make fundamental adjustments in the support contexts so that the children learn to communicate in ways that are in keeping with their cultural milieu.

■⊐ SUMMARY

A situated pragmatics approach necessitates that support be provided
that is consistent with the ways of the culture. This chapter reexamined
the six support contexts for how they may vary for children from different cultures. Some cultures have been found to emphasize group
over individual goals, thereby altering the nature of social support contexts. Affect is displayed and managed differently in different cultures
resulting in the need for reconceptualizing speech acts, or disputes, or
ways of saving face. Agendas are accomplished and interpreted in concert with the culture's mores and will differ for different cultures. Physical contexts will vary considerably depending on whether the child is

situated in an urban or rural context, and on whether the child is in a European or Asian tradition. Indeed, the ways of life will vary considerably with culture, requiring different approaches in keeping with the child's everyday experiences. Unless approaches are altered, those trying to use the situated pragmatics approach will find themselves unsituated, and the children they are serving are likely to feel alienated rather than supported.

Support in
School Contexts

Unbeknownst to most who design and carry out today's intervention approaches is the close connection between their efforts and those of John Dewey. At the beginning of this century, Dewey promoted educational programs designed to help children learn about their world through practical classroom activities. He proposed the use of manual training in schools to help children learn academics in a contextualized way; he emphasized the importance of having children understand the practical implications of what they are learning; and he advocated substituting a child-centered, project-oriented curriculum over one organized around "subject matter."

The contemporary approaches to language intervention that include educational settings are inadvertently paying homage to Dewey. Some classroom-based interventions are organized as simulations of everyday life situations following Dewey's (1938) philosophy which led to his advocacy of manual training. Language instruction for children with communication disorders is now being carried out in the classroom rather than in the "speech room" and in collaboration with the classroom teachers rather than by the clinician in isolation (Idol, Paolucci-Whitcomb, & Nevin, 1986; Miller, 1989; Nelson, 1989; Norris, 1989). The goals of some interventions have shifted from a focus on correct language, in the abstract, to appropriate language for the context (Creaghead, 1992).

Advocates of pragmatically based approaches promote less didactic, more egalitarian interactions in classrooms, providing children with opportunities to talk more and to have more say in what is going on (e.g., Calculator, 1986; Calculator & Jorgenson, 1991; Wilkinson, Milosky, & Genishi, 1986). This focus on getting children to participate spontaneously and on their own terms conforms to Dewey's emphasis on child-centered approaches. And, although Dewey was not concerned with children who were disabled, he would have approved of the current efforts of pragmatically oriented clinicians to be part of the effort of attaining social, communicative, and educational success for children who are being transitioned from segregated to included classrooms.

The situated approaches we have been describing call for supportive contexts tailored to meet the communicative needs of particular children. A clinician may select from among a number of approaches that are available. Some have been designed to facilitate children's social acceptance by peers in the context of the school classroom (e.g., Odom, Peterson, McConnell, & Ostrosky, 1990) and the playground (Haring & Lovinger, 1989). Others are designed to provide children with a greater variety of role responsibilities and more control over the classroom events (e.g., Johnson & Johnson, 1987). Still others focus on children's event learning (e.g., Creaghead, 1992). And there are programs that have promoted various types of discourse support for teachers to use to enhance the communicative participation and learning of their students (see Chapter 13, pp. 134–264 in Silliman & Wilkinson, 1991). In this chapter we will discuss the available programs in terms of the six supportive contexts that provide a frame for our situated pragmatic approach.

■ THE SOCIAL CONTEXT OF CLASSROOMS

What sort of social support contexts might be provided to help children with special needs become viable members of a mainstream classroom? Staff members at the Center for Integrated Education in Toronto have devised a procedure which they call MAPS, making action plans (Vandercook, York, & Forest, 1989). The MAPS procedure involves gathering a group of individuals who will work together to assume responsibility for the included child. The group, including peers, teachers, and family members, meets to develop a picture of the new student, with a focus on their hopes or "dreams" for an optimum outcome for the child in that classroom as well as their fears or "nightmares" for the worst-case scenarios. The group then develops an action plan for ways to assist that child to achieve the dreams and withstand or avoid the fears. Once the plan is implemented, the group or subgroups of the original group meet to evaluate how it is going. The group evaluates periods of the school day for whether the plan worked, and if not how things might be changed to make it work better for the focus child.

Other social support situations which have been studied are those in which peers have been trained to interact with children who are on the social periphery. Approaches have involved invitational procedures for initiating social interactions (Odom, Hoyson, Jamieson, & Strain, 1985); using social scripts to encourage interaction (Loveland & Tunali, 1991); creating collaborative groups wherein children are assigned social role responsibilities (Johnson & Johnson, 1987); helping children get rid of socially stigmatizing behaviors (Goldstein & Gallagher, 1992); and creating classroom rules that prohibit social exclusion (Paley, 1992). (See Chapter 3 for a discussion of the various ways of promoting social interaction.)

■❏ THE INTENTIONAL CONTEXT OF CLASSROOMS

Several researchers and clinicians have studied the intentional context of the classroom by analyzing what functions language serves for the students as well as the teachers. Wilkinson and Calculator (1982) examined the requests children made to obtain information or action from others in the classroom. They found that children's requests varied in their degree of directness, who they were aimed at, their sincerity, the way they were revised when the goals were not achieved, the way they fit the ongoing context, and how they were responded to. Requests were defined by these researchers as single-act intents.

Tough (1981) offered a departure from the single-act intent view by classifying together intents devoted to the same communicative goal. For example, a series of utterances together devoted to reporting an event would be classified together as a report. Tough's view of intentionality is thus in keeping with the notion of an overall agenda. (See Chapter 3 for an elaboration of the distinction between single-act intents and multiple acts accomplishing an intended agenda.) Tough discovered seven types of agendas which govern children's discourse in classrooms (see Table 7–1).

We have until now been describing children's intents in classroom situations. A second way that intentionality in classrooms has been studied is to focus on the strategies and goals evidenced by teachers. Silliman and Wilkinson (1991), when summarizing the literature on teacher

TABLE 7-1
Agendas Which Language Serves Students in Typical Elementary Classrooms.

1. Self-maintaining, maintaining the rights and interests of the self.

2. Directing, using language to direct one's own actions and the actions of other people.

3. Reporting, giving a commentary on past or present experiences.

4. Logical reasoning, using language to reason about experiences.

5. Predicting and anticipating, looking forward to future experiences.

6. Projecting, trying to understand how others feel, or examining situations outside one's own experience.

7. Imagining, building up an imagined scene through play or original story, or playing a role.

Source: From Tough, J. (1981). *A place for talk.* London, England: Ward Lock Educational in association with Drake Educational Associates.

strategies, identified a variety of ways teachers achieve their overall purpose which is to teach content while keeping children under control. In the beginning phase of teacher-controlled activities, teachers aim to "minimize misunderstanding of purpose of content" by introducing the activity, reviewing past activities, and relating new to old knowledge (Silliman & Wilkinson, 1991, p. 60). Teachers also want to achieve a smoothly running turn-taking structure, and to this end create turn-taking rules, which they monitor and reinforce throughout an activity (Eder, 1982).

■□ THE EMOTIONAL CONTEXT OF CLASSROOMS

Cazden (1988), in her important book on classroom discourse, emphasized the significance that language has for expressing children's personal identity. Contexts that allow positive expressions of a child's identity are likely to promote positive emotion, those that include elements of rejection or frustration for the child will have negative emotional valence. Children who find the classroom activities mysterious or confusing are cast in socially peripheral roles and are forced to learn in contexts of negative emotion. (See Paley, 1990, 1992, and 1994 for descriptions of marginalized children in her kindergarten classroom, and how she designed activities to promote their involvement.)

Teachers may be inadvertently creating emotionally negative experiences for children when they evaluate the children's verbal performances. The teacher's responses in the following exchange illustrate how a teacher who is trying to help a child arrive at a right answer, may be building a situation of negative emotion and a child. By contrast, in the second exchange, a child, Wally, offers a positive context of acceptance for his friend Rose.

Two Emotional Contexts:
One Negative and One Positive

A teacher evaluates an 8-year-old's discourse contributions:

Teacher:	Can you tell me, Ben, about all the things that were happening on the building site? What was the first thing we saw?
Ben:	The man digging.
Teacher:	No, I don't think that was the first thing, was it? What was the first thing?
Ben:	Bricks.
Teacher:	No, I don't think so.
Ben:	Was it a ladder.
Teacher:	There was something else first, just think.
Ben:	We went through a gate first.
Teacher:	Can't you remember? Well, there was a sign, wasn't there? What did it say?
Ben:	It had a name on.
Teacher:	Can you remember what the name was?
Ben:	It was John Somebody I think.
Teacher:	John Robinson & Sons, Building Contractors. I wonder what that means?
Ben:	They build things — houses.
Teacher:	Well, not just houses — what else could they build?
Ben:	Roads.

(Tough, 1981, pp. 80-81)

(continued)

A child makes sense of his friend's confusing discourse:

Lisa: 1. My daddy says black people come from Africa.

Wally: 2. I come from Chicago.

Lisa: 3. White people are born in America.

Wally: 4. I'm black and I was born in Chicago.

Rose: 5. Because more people come dressed up like they want to.

Wally: 6. How do they dress up?

Rose: 7. You know, like going to church or someplace.

Wally: 8. You mean if they're black?

Rose: 9. They can dress up like they want to.

Wally: 10. I see what she means.
          11. Like getting dressed up to go to church?

Rose: 12. Like they want to.

Wally: 13. Not in a black dress, right?
          14. You can wear a white dress?

Rose: 15. Yes.

(Paley, 1981, p. 47)

◼️ THE PHYSICAL CONTEXT OF CLASSROOMS AND PLAYGROUNDS

Classrooms and playgrounds are the living spaces for children when they are in school. The physical arrangement of playground equipment, chairs and tables, work and play spaces, and materials influences what children choose to do and how and when they do it. Also relevant for some children is whether there are spaces in classroom to which children can escape to be alone. Finally, there may be spaces, such as time-out chairs where children are instructed to go for punitive reasons. (See the dramatic differences between the two classrooms described in the following schools, the first representing a "hard school" atmosphere, the second one a "soft school" atmosphere.)

How Physical Space Can Exude Atmosphere for a School

The Hard Atmosphere:

A barred gate in a brick wall opens into an asphalt playground. A notice on the wall reads: bicycle riding, handball playing, hardball playing prohibited by the Toronto Board of Education. Fifth grade children are standing in groups, one or two are skipping. An electric bell rings and a teacher marshals the children into a line. They walk up three steps and enter the concrete school building . . . The children are led into a classroom and seated in alphabetical order at desk-chairs with built-in book racks.

(Barton, 1970b, p. 183)

The Soft Atmosphere:

Posters abound. Typewriters, paper, and pieces of circuitry litter the floor . . . In the heart of the confusion, a teacher is busy painting a mural of dinosaurs . . . Close by, there is a computer terminal, a refrigerator, and a large gas cooker, all in constant use.

(Barton, 1970b, p. 186)

Besides providing an overall atmosphere, the arrangement of objects offers explicit frameworks within which children carry out their activities. Here also classrooms can differ from ones with a physical context that is highly prescriptive to classrooms in which the children are invited to provide the structure. These two extremes are offered in excerpts that follow describing activities in which the physical context prescribes what is to take place, and activities that are highly open ended.

Physical Materials and Their Dictates

A restricted classroom activity:

Materials: A board depicting the sacred ball game, with spaces for moving pawns to a predetermined end (a

(continued)

hoop); a series of cards. Each card has an Aztec question on one side (e.g., "How did Aztec parents punish their children?") and three answers on the other. One answer is one topic (e.g., "Children were poked with cactus needles and thrown into a pool of ice-cold water"); another is tangential to the question content (related but not exactly on topic, e.g., "Children were considered disobedient if they did not follow parents' rules"); and the third is off topic (e.g., "The Aztec people got their food from farming").

(Silliman & Wilkinson, 1990, p. 91)

An open-ended classroom activity:

David Stanfield and I have been taking a box of multi-media materials on "The Thirties — The Age of the Great Depression" into school classrooms. It is one of our notions that disorganization has positive educational values. The contents of the box are disorganized, and when the children are using the box the classroom becomes disorganized . . . The materials in the box are soft in the sense that no attempt has been made to structure them. No labels on the records, no titles on the filmstrips, no captions on the slides, no step-by-step instructions for the student. Just $30 worth of raw materials: postcards, stamps, newspapers, letters, all mixed together: over a thousand items.

(Barton, 1970a, p. 195)

■❑ CLASSROOM AND PLAYGROUND EVENTS

One approach for supporting children's everyday communication is to take the events that take place as a point of departure. Classrooms often are organized around a repeating schedule of events. Playground activities are also likely to be highly structured. It is within these circumscribed events, whether they be lessons, projects, discussions, pretense, or games, that children with or without communicative disorders must operate. Some clinicians, teachers, and researchers have therefore advocated working with children in the contexts of classroom activities. For example, Creaghead (1992) has identified events which typically occur in preschools, primary, and upper grades in American mainstream schools. She has advocated viewing these events as scripts children need to learn in order to participate appropriately. (See Table 7–2 for a listing of common classroom activities for different children of different ages.)

Calculator and Jorgensen (1991) also addressed the need for designing intervention programs to fit children's daily activities. These authors focused their efforts on ways to integrate children with severe disabilities in regular education settings. They distinguish between functional goals, and those that are a step removed from their functional applications. They call the first "integrated objectives" and the second "nonintegrated objectives." For example, an integrated objective would be to have a child request help in getting onto a swing during recess, and a nonintegrated objective to have the child match a photograph to its corresponding real-world object (a picture of a spoon to an actual spoon). The context for integration, in this case, is the curriculum as defined by what is being done by other children in the class.

An extension of Calculator and Jorgensen's design of integrated goals has been laid out by Jorgensen (1992), who provides a myriad of ways for providing a child with needed support for participating in a mainstream curriculum. This approach epitomizes a philosophy of situated pragmatics, in that it takes the daily activities going on in the classroom as a point of departure for determining what support is needed by a child to participate in those events. The approach, developed by a group at the University of New Hampshire, is part of an inservice training project called INSTEPP (Integrating Neighborhood Schools: Training Educational Personnel and Parents). It involves analyzing a child's everyday participation in school events and summarizing the types of support provided. Included as part of the summary are the supports shown in the box on the next page.

TABLE 7–2
Typical School Events.

Preschool	Primary Grades	Middle and Upper Grades
Arriving	Reading group	Doing oral reports
Show and tell	Recess	Doing written reports
Snack time	Lunch	Test taking
Cleaning up	Doing homework	Following teacher lectures
Bathroom	Workbooks	(notetaking)
Story time	Art	Working with other students
Going home	Riding bus	Participating in discussions

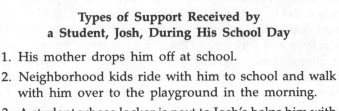

**Types of Support Received by
a Student, Josh, During His School Day**

1. His mother drops him off at school.

2. Neighborhood kids ride with him to school and walk with him over to the playground in the morning.

3. A student whose locker is next to Josh's helps him with his arrival routine.

4. A classroom teacher helps him with his lunch and personal belongings.

5. Students in his class help him find his writing folder, read with him during language arts time, help him with the Pledge of Allegiance, help him pretend to escape from Freddy Kruger, help him with his juice box and chips bag, help him contribute to the science activity, and teach him how to use a timer for knowing when activities are completed.

(Jorgensen, 1992, pp. 204–205)

Calculator and Jorgensen have taken as their aim teaching children how to understand and perform in daily activities carried out in the classroom. Other approaches have focused on enhancing children's communicative understandings during classroom activities. The enhancement takes place by providing them with feedback as the activities are being carried out. This focus uses the curriculum as a means for other sorts of learning rather than teaching children about the activities themselves. Norris (1989), for example, helps children develop their language understandings during classroom reading activities. The techniques, which she calls Communicative Reading Strategies (CRSs) (Norris, 1989), include (1) writing a segmented text for the child which includes a targeted language structure; (2) having the child read that portion of the text to others in the reading group; and (3) providing feedback to the child about success in using the targeted structure.

◼︎◻︎ THE DISCOURSE CONTEXTS OF CLASSROOMS AND PLAYGROUND

The events that take place during a school day provide opportunities for a variety of discourse genres. Activities of traditional classrooms are likely to differ from other life contexts in that they are more likely to be controlled by teachers whose aims are to achieve mutual attention between themselves and members of their classes (Merritt, 1982), as well as to help children learn from classroom discourse (Wilkinson & Calculator, 1982). For this reason, one finds a high proportion of classroom talk that is monitored and evaluated by the teacher, not only for its content but for its conformance to the rules for who can talk and at what times (Cazden, 1988; Eder, 1982).

A typical format for carrying out classroom discourse takes place in structured lessons. The structure is one in which the teacher initiates (I) an exchange, a student responds (R), and the teacher evaluates that response (E). This is the well-researched IRE exchange structure (Mehan, 1979; see Chapter 8 for a more "situated" view of this discourse genre and the IRE structure). In this format, children need help in understanding how and when to respond (Eder, 1982; Hood, McDermott, & Cole, 1980) and how to penetrate the structure if they want to say something outside the format or content of the lesson (Eder, 1982).

A second genre commonly found in classrooms is event description. Children in preschools are required to participate in a daily sharing time activity sometimes called "show and tell." Literacy activities in the early grades typically involve event descriptions. Children are asked to write about what they did last summer or what they did last night. A group effort may be one in which children dictate an "experience story" describing what happened on a field trip. In all these cases, parts of the event need to be extracted, described in past tense, and sequenced in logical and temporal order.

Students in the upper grades need to develop the ability to read and write expository discourse. Expository is the language typical of report writing, in which the student is required to create a coherent exposition having to do with a particular topic. Subjects such as science and social studies are often couched in expository discourse.

A fourth type of discourse has come to the fore with the advent of collaborative learning activities (Hill & Hill, 1990; Johnson & Johnson, 1987; Sharan & Sharan, 1992; Slavin, 1990). Here children are required to engage in mutual problem solving. They are assigned social roles such as leader or reporter and given a task to solve. The discourse required by this circumstance is likely to involve interactive negotiations, meta talk about what the roles entail, and a differentiation of the talk associated with the different roles.

Supporting children's discourse in classrooms can help them learn different discourse genres as well as whatever is conveyed within the genres. Helping children learn the nuances of the discourse genres peculiar to a specific classroom provides them with the knowledge they need to participate in those discourse contexts. Using familiar discourse contexts to support other learning provides children with a way to structure the new information. A language intervention program conducted during classroom activities can be structured differently depending on the particular intervention goals.

■◻ SITUATED PRAGMATICS AND CLASSROOM INCLUSION

Situated pragmatics approaches are the very ones often promoted by those working toward including children with severe disabilities in typical classrooms. The efforts are to provide support in whatever ways possible to create positive learning and social interactions in the context of the child's mainstream classroom. Jorgenson (1992), in Table 7–3 offers interesting indices for evaluating the success of the efforts of those who are working to make a child an active participant and social member of the class throughout the day.

■◻ SUMMARY

Classrooms are where school-age children spend much of their time. A situated pragmatic approach to facilitating children's development of communicative competence is thus compelled to consider how to support children's learning in the context of schools. We have discussed ways this support might be offered in focal areas of classroom activities: the social context, the intentional context, the emotional context, the physical context, the event context, and the discourse context. One important function of a situated approach is to provide children, who would in the past have been in special education classes, with the support needed so that they can be included in regular education.

TABLE 7-3
Indices of Whether Children with Disabilities Are Participating as Full Members in Schools and Classrooms.

Indicators of student being a true member of a school community:

1. Rides the same bus as typical students.
2. Uses the same facilities, rooms, resources as typical students.
3. Is eligible for election to the Student Council.
4. Is assigned to a grade, cluster, section, or homeroom like typical students.
5. Appears in photos in the yearbook.
6. Has a locker, coathook, or storage space in a typical location.
7. Is present at special events — graduation, plays, dances, sports events.

Indicators of full participation in a regular classroom:

1. Participates alongside typical peers in regular class lessons.
2. Goes on field trips to accessible places.
3. Is called on in class.
4. Participates in extracurricular activities.

Indicators of friendships:

1. Has friends (not just peer tutors or buddies).
2. Spends time with typical students after school and on weekends.
3. Gets telephone calls from friends at thome.
4. Hangs out with typical kids during school hours.
5. Is chosen by others for team memberships.

Source: From Jorgensen, C. (1992). Natural supports in inclusive schools, pp. 190, 193. In J. Nisbet (Ed.), *Natural supports in school, at work, and in the community for people with severe disabilities* (pp. 179–215). Baltimore, MD: Paul H. Brookes, with permission.

Situated Pragmatics in Its Own Context

How does situated pragmatics fit with other approaches in language intervention? By asking this question, we are evaluating situated pragmatics in light of its own context, that of the myriad other approaches designed to help children advance in their abilities to communicate together and with adults.

One can distinguish among the many approaches to language intervention the following six: (1) behavioral approaches (e.g., milieu teaching, social skills training); (2) linguistic approaches (e.g., teaching targeted structures in phonology, morphology, syntax, and semantics); (3) cognitive approaches (working on cognitive prerequisites to communication); (4) information processing approaches (e.g. memory training, comprehension monitoring); (5) abstract pragmatics approaches (e.g., targeting turn taking, and exchange structures); and (6) whole language approaches (e.g., focusing on thematic meanings and function).

The situated approach put forward in this book is significantly different from each of the six alternatives, and at the same time comparable to each in different ways. This chapter will outline the features of each of the six intervention approaches and examine how they are similar to and different from the situated pragmatics approach.

■□ BEHAVIORISM AND MILIEU TEACHING VERSUS SITUATED PRAGMATICS

The early behaviorists discussed in Chapter 1 have their progeny in today's proponents of behavioral techniques as applied to language intervention. The modern day version of behaviorism has moved in the direction of pragmatics in that the programs are often administered in the contexts of everyday activities and are organized to help the child achieve his or her communicative goals.

So, at first blush, the behavioral programs look similar to those developed using situated pragmatics. Adults following the milieu therapy approach create naturalistic contexts to facilitate, say, intents such as requests, and wait for the child to do something. They then model or expand on the child's response, reinforcing it to encourage the child to produce such responses in the future. What, then, distinguishes the approaches?

One major distinction is in how those engaged in the teaching view what they are doing. The behaviorist is helping the child form associations between stimuli, responses, and reinforcers. The teacher or clinician acting as a behaviorist is involved in acts of prompting, cuing, and reinforcing responses, and in breaking complex acts up into smaller, more learnable components.

A task analysis breaks a large task containing event or verbal chains into smaller elements that are related by virtue of their sequenced associations in the chain. Reinforcement is administered according to a well-planned schedule, proceeding from full to partial, from regular to random. Generalization involves a transfer of learned responses from the training context to other targeted contexts, and failure to generalize is taken to be a problem of stimulus or response associations between the learning and targeted contexts. An approach to aiding generalization is to train the child using multiple exemplars of the targeted structure (e.g., Stremel-Campbell & Campbell, 1985).

The teacher or clinician in the situated pragmatics paradigm provides the child with contextual support to help the child make sense of what is going on. The prompts need to be designed in the children's zone of understanding to aid them not only to respond appropriately, but to interpret what is happening around them. The children's actions are not seen as responses to stimuli, but as ways of conveying intents, carrying out agendas, or accomplishing an event. So the focus is not on providing them with the proper prompts or reinforcement but on helping them accomplish their goals and on engaging them in communicative exchanges or event sequences.

Situated pragmatics, rather than rendering a child's act as a response to an isolated stimulus, sees it as being an element in the context — an element that bears meaningful significance to other elements in that context. Further, a so-called stimulus takes on relevance not because it has intrinsic salience but rather because it is meaningful in light of the child's background knowledge, current expectations, or because something in the current context is calling attention to it. The stimulus, then, should not be treated apart from the sense the child makes of it. That sense derives heavily from what the child is currently thinking — a mental source. Discriminative stimuli are therefore misnamed, and should instead be called **meaningful elements**.

Sequences of responses cast as behavioral chains in the behavioral framework are seen in the situated pragmatics framework as a set of planned actions governed by goal structures or subscripts within a larger script. So brushing ones teeth, regarded by behaviorists as a chain, becomes a meaningful activity to a situated pragmatist, with subparts that bear a logical relation to one another. (Taking a cap off the toothpaste enables one to get the paste out.) A pragmatist who approaches a task analysis would consider the variety of meaningful relations which the performer of the task sees among the steps in the task. The job of the learner is not seen as memorizing separated steps, but rather as learning the meaningful relations of each subpart to the whole task — as a dynamic, active and creative exercise in sensemaking.

Situated pragmatics substitutes meaningful feedback for reinforcement. The mechanisms for feedback may not be ones that immediately follow the targeted response, but instead ones that continue through several turn exchanges. For example, when a child fails to achieve a communicative goal he or she might retry, or **repair** the communicative failure. The literature on repairs has revealed that, when the breakdown causes a misunderstanding on the part of the listener, the child speaker is likely to make a new attempt — often closer to the adult language (e.g., Weiner & Ostrowski, 1979). This research finding on revisions requires a reinterpretation of the ultimate efficacy of intermittent reinforcement programs that provide no information about why certain actions sometimes work and sometimes fail.

The pragmatics notions of **event structure** and **sensemaking** also lead to a reevaluation of the behavioral notion of reinforcement contingencies. An event that regularly calls for a reinforcement turn from the clinician falls into the genre of "lesson" (Mehan, 1979) in that each reinforcement has an evaluative function. Said more concretely, reinforcement, when made explicit, may change an event from a child-centered one to a teacher-centered one. A clinician following a child's lead during play undermines the child's control by evaluating the child's performance during that play. Furthermore, if the child's agenda for an event is something other than earning reinforcers, introduction of periodic reinforcers into that event is likely to alter the original event.

Problems with generalization are viewed pragmatically as involving sensemaking — perhaps the child places the teaching context in one frame and the generalization context in another. Or maybe the child interprets a new exemplar of a formed concept using another schema, and that is why generalization fails to take place. So, the recommendation of providing the child with multiple examples of a targeted concept needs to be evaluated in the light of what those examples mean to the child. If the new example or the context of generalization fits a different schema, generalization is not likely to take place. If, on the other hand, the new example or generalization situation is seen by the child as a logical extension of the old, it will be readily understood and generalization will appear to have taken place.

Finally, as is argued elsewhere in this book, the way an individual makes sense of what is going on will inevitably alter what that person does. This is the also case when that individual is the clinician. A behaviorist-clinician who fails in his or her aim to get the child to issue a request will tell the child what to say. If the child fails to imitate, the clinician may move on to another item in the training program. A clinician thinking within the framework of situated pragmatics will tell the child what to say in contexts where he or she can safely assume what the child wants to say (when the child is in an intentional state that fits the words). If the child says "I want paint" in a context where he wants a cookie, the training item has not been well conceived. Further, if the child does not request something, the pragmatist may try to determine why, on this occasion, a previously desirable item is not being requested. Maybe the child is not hungry, maybe he wants something else.

■◻ LINGUISTIC APPROACHES VERSUS SITUATED PRAGMATICS

Linguistic approaches to intervention take as the primary enterprise the teaching of linguistic concepts, usually rules. (See Connell, 1982, and the following box for an illustration of this approach). The clinician targets one or two linguistic units to work on and presents a child with structures manifesting that unit. If a child substitutes stops for fricatives, the clinician may bombard the child with words containing fricatives and provide the child with practice saying fricatives in syllables or words.

The program may proceed from working on fricatives in isolated words to saying fricatives in phrases and sentences. This approach resembles the "Van Riper" approach to articulation training (Van Riper, 1963), but is informed by more recent influences from linguistics that treats similar sounds as part of a feature or process category in language system (e.g., phonological processes).

An Example of the Linguistic View of Language

Language is composed of a complex set of interrelated rules. Language consists of several types of rules which specify the distribution of sounds, morphemes, words, phrases, and clauses in sentences and which specify the meaning associated with these elements and their various possible distributions. The importance of rules, especially at the syntactic level of language, is that they specify the distribution of grammatical categories. The rules explicitly describe the context of environments in which linguistic elements may occur and, by inference, those in which such elements may not occur. Consequently, to learn a rule, the learner must become aware of the linguistic contexts or environments which obligate and element as well as those which preclude an element: The learner must recognize the conditions which control the use or occurrence of the elements.

(Connell, 1982, p. 231)

Linguistic therapy also involves teaching inflectional morphemes and syntactic rules as discrete elements, beginning with sessions in which the child is presented with multiple examples of the targeted forms (called "focused stimulation" by Fey, 1986). The children then are asked or encouraged to produce their own examples of the rule and provided along the way with feedback about how they are doing.

Linguistic approaches were especially popular in the 1980s. Advocates of those linguistic approaches, many of whom are currently pioneering approaches that move us toward situated pragmatics, targeted linguistic structures as the goal of learning. They created innovative pragmatic approaches for teaching such structures that involved departing from the traditional lesson or game format, and modeling and eliciting the structures in contexts that simulate everyday-life. Constable (1983) and Culatta (1984), for example, recommended the use of pretend play contexts during which clinicians bombard the child with targeted linguistic forms, elicit those forms from the child, and model the correction after the child produces the forms.

Areas of pragmatics can also be couched in more traditional linguistic-like frameworks. That is, they can be treated as discrete rule-like structures that exist in a knowledge system, separate from the context, and retrieved when needed. So children are taught how to initiate topics, take turns, and request objects or actions. Clinicians subscribing to this linguistic view of pragmatics may create language programs that offer children multiple examples of the target, elicit and model the children's productions, and provide the children with feedback to help them evaluate their productions (e.g., Olswang, Kriegsmann, & Mastergeorge, 1982).

The situated pragmatics view of language differs from the linguistic view in a variety of ways. First, rather than assuming that language is separable from its contexts, the situated pragmatics view would argue that language is but one part of what goes on in communication, and that it is inseparable from the other parts.

This notion of interrelatedness of language and its contexts of use is consistent with the **functionalist view** of language presented by Bates and MacWhinney (1987) and Leonard and Fey (1991), among others. Functionalists see language as being in the service of communication goals — first words are learned in order to accomplish speech acts of requesting and commenting; interrogatives that include "wh" question forms are used to ask questions, connectives indicate to the partner how to relate an upcoming clause to the preceding discourse, relative clauses help differentiate more focused from lesser focused information, advanced vocabulary is needed to be able to talk about or reference what is important and interesting to oneself and others. Children also use the support of the surrounding discourse to structure their learning and use of language (Leonard & Fey, 1991). So when a program is designed to teach children language structure without concern for how those structures serve the child's communicative needs, it is missing an important ingredient. One might argue that this omission may cause what has come to be known as the "carryover problem" for clinicians — children may be able to use their new learnings in a teaching situation, but fail to carry their use into the contexts of everyday communication.

A second major difference between linguistic and situated pragmatics approaches is in the domain of meaning interpretation. Linguistic approaches look for meaning in the elements of the language — the words convey lexical meaning, the sentences convey propositional meaning, the discourse has cohesion via meaning relationships between clauses and words in different sentences (a closed text view). Situated pragmatics locates meaning in the thought of the language users as they go about making sense of what is taking place. The event situated in its physical and emotional context is put together with the discourse and language structure to create an overall understanding.

A third difference between linguistic and situated pragmatic views of communication lies in how one goes about determining which units of communication to focus on. The linguistic view is likely to place primary emphasis on the linguistic aspects of communication: sounds, words, phrases, sentences, and how these units fit together into a predictable discourse structure. To teach children how to communicate in a more adult-like way, they must learn these elements and how they combine. The co-occurrences of elements are dictated by the linguistic rules.

The situated pragmatics view would place the sensemaking enterprise as central and most influential in determining how to break up the situation into its component parts. Units of language may be understood as those that serve the same function (e.g., discourse markers), those that can be substituted for one another in events or discourse (e.g., greetings), and those that are identified with roles (e.g., evaluative comments). Children's understanding and use of linguistic elements may change with different registers, different partners, and different events.

Finally, a linguistic approach to intervention would focus on teaching children language rules, whereas a situated pragmatics approach would focus on providing support contexts for facilitating communication. The effort of the first is to teach children what they need to know about language, the second is to help them discover and use what they need to know to communicate in contexts of everyday life.

■□ COGNITIVE APPROACHES VERSUS SITUATED PRAGMATICS

Cognitive approaches to language intervention have, like situated pragmatics approaches, emphasized the things children need to know about the world to communicate meaningfully in it. Some cognitive approaches focus on precursors to language learning. For example, there are programs dedicated to helping children who do not yet understand symbols to attain symbolic understanding (for a review see Owens, 1991, pp. 286–290) and programs dedicated to helping children move from a concrete to abstract way of thinking, sometimes called decentering (Norris & Hoffman, 1993a). We will take the concrete to abstract focus as our point of departure as we discuss the differences between cognitive and situated pragmatics approaches to language intervention.

The beginning communicator has been depicted as being context bound. Piaget (1954), for example, described young children as being centered in the presenting occasion and unable to decenter or take an external perspective on what is happening. The result is, or so it is claimed, that the children live in the present.

The notion that first learnings are based in the here and now carries with it the common notion that young children or those who are severely mentally challenged are able to handle the manipulable, observable concrete better than they are more abstract and less tangible concepts. Clinicians therefore often use objects and pictures in their work with beginning language learners to start at the level of concrete learning with the hope of progressing toward the more abstract, once the proper foundation is laid.

The palpable, observable world is seen by adults as being comprised of perceivable things or actions. So language programs have been designed which have the child label objects or pictures and describe single actions or a series of pictures showing action sequences (Gillham, 1979; Simon, 1980). Programs with a more pragmatic focus have presented the child with tempting situations consisting of unreachable objects or difficult to manipulate toys so that children will ask for help (Bricker & Cripe, 1992; Hart & Rogers-Warren, 1978). Clinicians using pragmatic approaches based in concrete experiences have enacted with children an everyday scenario to provide them with a current context to hear modeled talk and to practice their own talking (Culatta, 1994; Norris & Hoffman, 1993a; Sonnenmeier, 1994).

Several theoreticians and researchers have questioned the view that a naive child's world is made up mostly of isolable, tangible, and observable objects, pictures, and actions. For example, Nelson (1973, 1991b) has been arguing for some time that, before children are able to isolate experiential episodes into their elemental parts (e.g., see a ball as separable from the game of throwing), they conceive the world as event episodes or scripts. A hole is to dig, objects are to play with in certain ways, with certain people, under prescribed circumstances.

Bloom and her colleagues (Bloom, Beckwith, & Capatides 1988; Bloom & Capatides, 1987), taking a slightly different tack, have suggested that first experiences are fused with affect and that tangible objects are identified as pleasurable or not, depending upon their affective history. First words, according to Bloom, grow out of a child's well developed mental representations of affective experiences. She argues from her research on the relationship between first words and expressions of affect that the child's earliest words are more than labels of concrete objects. They are also expressions of emotional content, as evidenced by the frequency with which children's nonverbal expressions of emotion follow their expressions of first words.

Gopnik (1982) has also concluded from her examination of children's first words that young children are not just interested in objects but also in how those objects fit into their own goals and plans for those objects. Gopnik observed that children had expressions among their first words which indicated that they were finished with doing something ("there") or that their goals were thwarted ("oh dear" or "no").

Another source of evidence that argues against the notion that concrete objects and isolated pictures are a good source for developing children's concrete knowledge comes from the analyses of children's picture books carried out by Perry Nodelman (1988). Nodelman examined a variety of picture books that are popular in the United States and found that even the simplest alphabet book created conceptual dilemmas that must be solved by the children when deciphering meaning from the pictures.

Analysis of Children's First Picture Books

The distance of this operation from the information the eye actually presents is made clear by the fact that in *A First Book Open and Say*, the depicted objects float on solidly colored backgrounds, so that there are no size cues and no sense of relative proportion; one spread depicts both a toy top and a house as about the same size, and the lack of visual cues makes it hard to determine whether it is meant to be a toy house or a real one. Furthermore, while none of the pictures depicts shadows and most are head-on views with no sense of depth, those of the top and of shoes imply a different angle of vision that suggest the depth of perspective drawing.

(Nodelman, 1988, p. 28).

An already accepted alternative to the view that objects and pictures are basic and concrete is the popular literature which casts certain toy objects as dangerous to children's psyches and to the society as a whole. For example, Sutton-Smith (1986) reviewed newspaper and television reports of concerns about the negative influences on children that toys such as Barbie dolls and toy guns could have. He found a common worry that these toys, because of what they symbolize in the culture, may have a profound negative effect on the socialization of young children (Sutton-Smith, 1986). In this view, the concrete objects are much more mean-

meaningful to children than would be ordinarily presumed. They are a means of socialization, a source of affection, an entry of the child into what is emphasized in the host culture.

Similarly, concerns have been commonly expressed about the profound effects of pictures on children's socialization. For example, when pictures show people engaged in activities, they specify certain people and particular activities. This specificity can convey to children that only certain people, say those of the mainstream culture, can engage in them; that the activities are gender-specific, or that other activities or scenes are not depicted in the pictures and by their absence convey a negative bias.

A Psychoanalyst's Comments on the Profound Meanings That Objects Can Have For Typical Infants

They (mothers) tell me about all sorts of objects which become adopted by the infant, and which become important, and get sucked or hugged, and which tide the infant over moments of loneliness and insecurity, or provide solace, or which act as a sedative. The objects are halfway between being part of the infant and part of the world.
(Winnicott, 1993, p. 16)

In sum, clinicians have long used objects, pictures, or enacted action sequences as props for structuring language activities. These activities are used to teach children object concepts, object and action names, inflectional morphology, and temporal sequencing. The assumption is that the provision of a stimulus without surrounding context makes it more graspable, more identifiable, and less confusing.

But what also needs to be considered is that isolating elements from their contexts changes them. Indeed, presenting a picture of a duck to a child for the child to identify, requires not only naming the picture, but also figuring out the relationship between the picture and one's world experience — a task that is neither concrete, nor located in the physical here and now of the language intervention session.

Further, the situations for learning names of objects, pictures, or actions are quite divorced from the situations in which that knowledge is used. The duck in a picture is quite different from the duck in a park. In the park the duck is understood as part of the scene, as part of an outing event, as something that makes sense in a context which is important to understanding what the word means. For the child to hear the word "duck" in the park is likely to be exciting and noteworthy. For the child to say the word "duck" when he sees it is likely to be interpreted as "look at that duck" or "I see a duck" whereas saying it in a classroom about a picture will be interpreted as "I know the name of that pictured animal."

So, rather than assuming that items isolated from context are likely to be easier to understand because they are concrete, we are arguing that they might be harder to understand because they lack the physical context needed to understand their meaning. Natural situations provide a richer context that helps children conjure up complex understandings that include not only the objects but the feelings, events, stories, and scenes associated with them. The situated pragmatics approach thereby offers the child contexts for learning that are more understandable because they are more situated.

■□ INFORMATION PROCESSING VERSUS SITUATED PRAGMATICS APPROACHES

The very way we construe communication reflects the strong influence that information processing theory has on how we go about teaching children to communicate. Traditional notions are based in what has come to be called a **conduit metaphor** (Duchan, 1994a; Lakoff, 1987; Reddy, 1979). The metaphor casts communication as an act of message sending, with a speaker sending the message to a listener and the listener receiving, interpreting, and responding to it. The conduit view gives short shrift to any of the types of situatedness emphasized in the situated pragmatics view. For example, it has little to say about how social or emotional context affects what is communicated; nor does it lead to an understanding of the role of the event or discourse contexts except that they somehow "contain" or "surround" or provide a frame or "scaffold" for communication.

Language intervention in the conduit framework involves providing the proper prompt to stimulate message formulation or sending, and the proper feedback to the child for a sent message. Methods, designed to cue or model what the child should say, are understood by clinicians as parts of a conduit metaphor.

An alternative view of communication, and one more in keeping with the situatedness of the approach presented in this book, is that it involves collaborations between and among communicative partners. Those involved work together to achieve an event, to create discourse, to socialize, and to accomplish goals. The **collaborative view** of communication is contrasted with the conduit view in Table 8–1.

The conduit view of communication characteristic of the information processing view has in it a representation of how language ia under-

TABLE 8-1
Differences Between the Conduit and Collaborative Views of Communication.

	Conduit View	Collaborative View
Participants are:	Speakers and listeners	Communication partners
Messages are:	Formulated by speakers and sent to them by listeners	Co-constructed
Teachers provide:	Cuing, prompting, and reinforcement	Mutual referencing and support
Conversations involve:	Turn taking between partners	Social interaction
Partners:	Follow conversational rules	Engage in conversation
Nonverbal behaviors:	Are signals sent from one to the other	Allow for co-participation
Events are:	Contexts for communication	Communication achievements
Language is:	A conduit for expressing messages	A part of sensemaking

stood once it is received. The language, cast as information strings, is passed through a series of steps, either serial or parallel, in which it is processed into meaningful components. Once processed the information is stored for later use. On the production side of processing, the information processing view requires that a potential speaker formulate a message by retrieving the needed information from the storage system and passing it through a variety of networks (syntax, semantics, phonology, speech production) and articulating it in serial order for a listener's reception.

Important in the processing are subsystems having to do with, for example, attention, memory, speech reception, and speech production systems. Language intervention programs designed for children with problems in these areas are based on the assumption that, unless a child's processing abilities are intact, the children will have problems in learning and using language.

The situated pragmatics approach argues alternatively that programs focusing on processing without proper attention to meaning and use in everyday life are met with the same difficulties that occur for any approach that works outside the sensemaking context. The remedy is that children with problems attending, remembering, perceiving, or producing language be provided with training that is situated and meaningful for them, and that didactic programs designed to teach processing are likely to achieve greater success when presented as child-centered programs to support processing in everyday life contexts.

■□ ABSTRACT VERSUS SITUATED PRAGMATICS APPROACHES

A typical discourse pattern said to be used in middle-class American homes and to be indicative of an instructional sequence in American schools is the initiation-response-evaluation or IRE exchange sequence. Specifically, a teacher (whether it be a parent, sibling, or classroom teacher) asks a child a question, the child responds, and the teacher evaluates the response. This IRE exchange pattern has been found to typify what people see as a school lesson (Cazden, 1988; Mehan, 1979; Silliman & Wilkinson, 1991). The IRE has also been identified as a form frequently used in clinical interactions between speech-language pathologists and their child clients (Becker & Silverstein, 1984; Prutting, Bagshaw, Goldstein, Juskowitz, & Umen, 1978, reviewed in Duchan, 1993a). Children who have had speech or language therapy can use the pattern both when they play the role of a child respondent and when they pretend to be the "speech teacher" (Ripich & Panagos, 1985).

If the above literature is an accurate rendition for what goes on in classrooms and many clinical interactions, it follows that the IRE structure is a exchange pattern that occurs often in the child's life. It is therefore a possible structure to target for children who are found to have difficulty in following the IRE exchange. An abstract pragmatics framework would see this structure as an isolated phenomenon that repeats over and over again as a turn-taking exchange structure typical in classroom lessons. A situated pragmatics approach requires that this structure be examined in light of other contexts as well as the context of turn-taking. Both views lead to the conclusion that the IRE exchange structure needs to be learned. They differ in what they think needs to be learned. The abstract pragmatics view treats the structure as a three-part event, and one that is relatively simple. The situated pragmatics approach sees the IRE pattern as highly complex and one that requires considerable savvy about various aspects of what is going on in lessons. Thus, a situated view makes the abstract view look as if it is misconstruing the IRE exchange in a variety of ways.

Six examples are outlined below, cast as myths about the nature of the IRE sequence.

Myth 1: IREs are simple, sequential structures, easily recognizable, with minimum room for variability

The IRE sequence is often portrayed as a easily identifiable triad, and one that is concrete and repetitive so that children can be provided with a structure for learning. But is it so simple? Let's examine each of the three elements to see what allows them to be identified.

Initiations

A question, say one that asks about what time it is, may or may not be an part of an IRE structure. It may be seen as a real request for information and not a test question whose answer will be evaluated. For an initiation such as a question to be recognized as the first move in a lesson, the respondent must infer that the requester is soliciting a response. A comment may sometimes be intended as an indirect initiation in an IRE sequence and at other times simply be a observation (e.g., It's going to snow today and it's May already. Isn't that strange?)

Initiations vary in how closely they tie to preceding discourse context. When several IRE sequences follow one another and bear little resemblance to each other in content, they have been called "discrete point" sequences (e.g., "What's this?" [shows cup]. "And what's this" [shows   car]).

Initiations may vary in the degree to which they constrain the following response. The less constraining initiations have been called "open," the more constraining have been called "closed."

Initiations aimed at testing what a child knows have been called "right answer questions" or "test questions" (e.g.,"What did the boy do then?"). Those designed to elicit unknown information for further evaluation have been called "authentic" or "real" questions (e.g., "What do you think he will do now?").

Initiations may be topical (e.g., "Why do you think the Statue of Liberty is green?") or they may be procedural (e.g., Do you really mean an m?). In the first case, they have to do with the meanings being created in the lesson, in the second how the lesson is getting carried out (Sonnenmeier, 1993).

Initiations may be directed to a particular addressee (e.g., John?), to a group of children (e.g., "What do you think, group 3?), or to a general audience (Who knows the answer?).

Responses

A response, in order to qualify as such, must be related in content to the initiation. To be judged as "appropriate" or "correct," responses need to fit what the initiator expects.

A response may also serve as an initiation. Mehan (1979) identified the contribution of Prenda in the sequence in the following box as an initiation, whereas Cazden (1988) classifies it as a response to the teacher's earlier question. We agree with both, as would Kaye and Charney (1981) who classify elements such as this "turnabouts." They interface with the previous elements as responses and with the subsequent elements as initiations.

An IRE Exchange Where the Starred Element Is Both a Response and an Initiation

I *Teacher:* (in a discussion about the location of Arkansas): And, Carolyn, how did you remember where it was? Its kind of in the middle of the country and hard to find out.

R *Carolyn:* Uh, cuz, cuz, all three of the grandmothers cuz, cuz, Miss Coles told us to find it and she said it started with an A and I said there (pointing) and it was right there.

R I* *Prenda:* Rhode Island

E *Teacher:* Yes, and I thought maybe you remembered because, Carolyn, you mentioned Little Rock yesterday.

(Cazden, 1988, p. 36)

Evaluations

Evaluations may be cast as positive or negative. Some evaluations may provide further information about the topic or theme (e.g., Response: "She saw the wolf in the bed." Evaluation: "Uh huh, she thought it was her grandmother, didn't she?").

Evaluations are optional. However, when they are absent, the responder may infer them and even infer whether the absent element is positive or negative. For example, if the teacher asks another child to answer the same question, one can infer a negative evaluation. If she goes on to another question, one can infer a positive evaluation.

Evaluations may be made in the same frame as the topic (e.g., "Yes, he never should have done that") or can shift to a meta-level outside the frame of the discussion (e.g., "great answer, Clyde").

Myth 2: The person with power does the initiating and evaluating and the less powerful person does the responding

IREs are usually treated as didactic forms to be avoided in a more child-centered approach because the clinician or teacher wields too much power. The question can be raised, then, about whether the IRE, by its very structure, assigns power.

Consider a courtship interaction where the partner who is courting asks the questions and evaluates the answer and the partner being courted is powerfully reticent, or consider a child who refuses to perform for the parent who thereby gains power in the situation. Fishman (1978) argues from data between male and female intimate couples that the powerless person often is the one who does the "work" in an interaction by initiating the topic, and keeping the event moving along, whereas the powerful person may take a role of a respondent, accruing power by virtue of a lack of enthusiasm about having to respond.

Myth 3: IREs are obvious and do not need to be interpreted

In the last example, the starred response made by the child was regarded by the teacher as an answer to her previous question — as a response. The analyst (Mehan, 1979) treated it as an initiation, where a new topical element was introduced. An argument can be made from this difference that the same element can serve multiple roles in an IRE sequence. Participants in the exchange may regard an element differently depending on their construal of the situation, topic, or history. In the following example, the teacher used a question to get a child to initiate. The teacher did not regard the question as being its own initiation (Kovarsky & Duchan, 1992). Rather, she took the effort as one which involved child-centered therapy exchanges different from the more traditional teacher directed therapies:

Teacher:	Now who wants hit?
Child:	Give me the stick.
Teacher:	(gives the child a stick)

Onlookers examining the exchange felt the teacher's question was an initiation and the child's utterance was a response. Compliance on the part of the teacher then becomes an evaluation of the child's response rather than the teacher's response to the child's command. This ambiguity in how to read the exchange is likely to affect the way the participants regard the overall event, and the power relations between those carrying it out. For example, the child in the above example may or may not have wanted the stick. If not, the elicitation on the part of the teacher is seen as a summons, as an act of power requiring a response that was forced. If so, the child may have issued the request, regardless of his own desire.

Myth 4: IREs are peculiar to lessons and do not occur in conversations

Rather than view the IRE as a structure that typifies the discourse of lessons, one might better regard it as an exchange structure that commonly occurs in a variety of discourse contexts. The difference between lessons and other genres may be that a lesson is more likely to have closed questions with right answers and evaluations based on accuracy. Conversations that contain IREs are likely to have IREs with open questions, unexpected responses and evaluations related to content rather than meta evaluations having to do with the skill of the responder. Table 8–2 illustrates the IRE exchange structure under conditions of highly constrained lessons and more open-ended conversations.

Myth 5: The IRE, because it is simple and obvious, is not likely to be influenced by overarching ideologies

In the United States learning to communicate is viewed from a *behavioral framework*, a framework that brings with it certain assumptions. Children are depicted as learning language by hearing it from those around them. The most frequently heard structures are the ones most likely to be learned first and best. Rehearsal via practice is crucial to language learning. The most frequently used structures are bound to be best learned. And the structures most rewarded through positive reinforcement are likely to be the strongest. This stimulus-response-reinforcement paradigm is a pervasive cultural schema held by lay people as well as professionals and scholars.

The three-part IRE structure reflects the way we, as members of the mainstream American culture, think of communication in general. The

TABLE 8-2
IREs as They May Occur in Different Discourse Genres.

IRE Sequence	Lesson	Conversation

I	Closed
	Answer known to issuer
	Purpose to test
	    competence
		More open
		Answer not known
		Purpose to find out
		    something or social

R	Right answer Closed choice set	Opinion (e.g., choice) Open choice set

E	Evaluation of performance
	Evaluation of accuracy
	Can result in
	    embarrassment
	If not present, implied and
	    supplied
		Continuation of information
		    exchange
		Not usually related to face
		    saving
		If not present, not implied or
		    supplied

construction presumes the conduit metaphor, rather than the collaborative view we are arguing for. Rather than seeing an exchange involving three separable components and comprised of messages sent by different partners, the collaborative view would cast the participants as working together to pose questions, to add to the topic, and to give one another feedback about how interpretations mesh with intended meanings. The collaboration involves overlapping of the three elements of the structure, wherein responses can influence what is asked, feedback can be provided by both partners all along the exchange, and initiations also serve as responses to previous exchanges or as ways of giving feedback. There may be a number of moves within each of the slots of the IRE, and each move may have several functions. A move may influence other moves which have yet to be produced as well as ones to follow.

The collaborative view of an IRE exchange would change its nature. Table 8–3 lists a variety of ways the IRE would be changed under the collaborative view.

Myth 6: IREs are exchange structures that have little to do with the cultural context

In most discussions of IRE structuring there no mention is made of how the structure fits with the interactional patterns to which the children from different cultures are accustomed. However, there is an alternative

TABLE 8-3
Ways the Collaborative View of the IRE Exchange Structure Would
Change One's View of It.

I = Both partners collaborate to form an initiation:

The issuer designs the solicitation to fit with what the rescipient knows, and with their past history.

The recipient provides interactive feedback during the issuance of the initiation, providing opportunities to change the initiation during its formation.

Previous discourse allows the recipient to solicit the initiation from a partner:

Know what?

You'll never guess what happened to me.

Predicted discourse influences how questions might get asked (e.g., trying to encourage a performance from an unwilling respondent).

There may be IREs within the I slot in slowed-down discourse or when the partners have a communication breakdown (e.g., I = What did you say? R = XXX. E = Oh.).

R = The partners collaborate to form a response:

The responder takes the content and presuppositions from the initiator to form the questions.

The responder selects the response based upon what the initiator must be thinking or wanting.

The responder and initiator communicate during the formation of the response adjusting what is done based on one another's signaling (perhaps using embedded IREs).

Responses are often co-constructed with people finishing one another's sentences, and cutting each other off, or talking over one another, or interpreting what is being said and done idiosyncratically.

E = Evaluations are made by the issuer in accordance with what he or she thinks the responder might take to be meaningful:

Evaluations made in public are interpreted by both initiator and responder in light of possible reactions of onlookers (e.g., maintaining face, losing face).

Evaluations can be made nonverbally during the production of the response as well as in the exchange slot following the response.

Self-evaluations are sometimes permissible and evaluations may be solicited by the responder (e.g., How did I do?).

---

literature, which does not directly discuss the IRE lesson-format but has implications for it. The literature is based on ethnographic approaches to the study of children's ability to succeed in school. For example, some researchers have found that conversational participation structures of home cultures to strongly affect children's performance in school (Au, 1980; Heath, 1982, 1983; Tharp & Gallimore, 1988).

Drawing from the ethnographic data, one would expect that children's ability to conform to an IRE lesson will depend on their home culture's interactional norms. Some cultures, for example, do not tie children's learning to adult teaching. Heath (1983), in her description of an African-American cultural group that lives in the Piedmont mountains of the Carolinas, described their preference for children's undirected discovery as a way for them to find out about the world. Heath contrasted that indirect approach to learning, which is incompatible with an IRE formatted learning experience, with a second cultural group, white families of nearby Roadville, who subscribe to the directive style of learning for their children. The following box contains comments of mothers from each group reflecting the two styles.

Two Views of How Children Learn

A Trackton mother subscribes to an indirect approach to learning, one incompatible with IRE exchanges:

He gotta learn to know 'bout dis world, can't nobody tell 'im. Now just how crazy is data? White folks uh hear dey kids say sump'n, day say it back to 'em, dey aks 'em 'gain 'n 'gain 'bout things, like dey 'posed to be born knowin'. You You think I kin tell Teegie all he gotta know to get along? He just gotta be keen, keep his eyes open, don't he be sorry. Gotta watch hisself by watchin' other folks. Ain't no use me tellin' 'im: "Learn dis, learn dat. What's dis? What's dat?

(Heath, 1983, p. 84)

A Roadville mother's educational philosophy is more in keeping with the IRE direct approach to teaching:

I figure it's up to me to give 'im a good start. I reckon there's just some things I know he's gotta learn, you know, what things are, and all that. 'n you just don't happen onto doin' all that right.

(Heath, 1993, pp. 127–128)

A second finding in the ethnographic literature is that some cultures avoid negative evaluations of performance, so as not to embarrass the one being evaluated. Eriks-Brophy and Crago (1993), for example, have revealed an absence of evaluation in teacher-student interactions among members of the Inuit culture. In classrooms taught by Inuit teachers they found that the teachers did not ask particular children for specific answers, but rather addressed the questions (the I in an IRE sequence) to a group of children. Further, if a child responded incorrectly, the teacher did not evaluate negatively, but instead expanded on the child's answer. Only later, and unobtrusively, did the teacher talk to the child about a "wrong" answer.

Eriks-Brophy and Crago (1993) offer an interesting suggestion, that the Inuit style of interaction be adapted for use in clinical interactions, and be substituted for the tutorial initiation-response-evaluation exchanges. "Such an approach may reduce the feelings of resistance, depression, and/or low self-esteem which students involved in remedial processes often exhibit" (p. 15).

■□ SITUATED PRAGMTICS VERSUS WHOLE-LANGUAGE APPROACHES

The "whole" in whole language is an appeal by its proponents to take language as a whole, and not as a set of discrete elements added together as a whole. The whole language approach is most commonly associated with literacy and is a counter to phonics approaches to teaching reading (Norris & Damico, 1990). Goodman (1986) has called the phonics method of matching letters with sounds a "flat earth view of the world" (p. 37).

The whole language approach to teaching reading is the written modality counterpart to situated pragmatics. Whole language, like situated pragmatics, values contextualized learning. Edelsky, Altwerger, and Flores (1991) make their biases known by asking the difference between having a child read a word on a flash card and having a child read a word on a bumper sticker.

**Context Provided A Beginning Reader
Who Is Learning To Recognize Single Words**

Take the difference between a one-word bumper sticker and a one-word flash card. With the bumper sticker there

(continued)

are pragmatic clues (placement on the car) to permit guessing another pragmatic cue — the genre (bumper sticker). The genre in turn predicts yet another pragmatic cue — the purpose(s) . . .

What about the one-word flash card? The pragmatic cue is there — that is, the genre is flash card. So is the graphic cue — one word . . . Entire systems of cues are missing. The flash card can be any word. The one on the bumper sticker can't. The bumper sticker can be read: the flash card can only have tricks done with it — decoding tricks, letter-naming tricks.

(Edelsky, Altwerger, & Flores, 1991, p. 21)

Whole language includes in its philosophy many of the areas discussed in this book under situated pragmatics. Its name conjures up the relationship between whole units and their subparts — between a whole unit of discourse such as a child's story in a book and the elements that make up the story (pages, sentences, phrases, graphemes). The whole language equivalent in oral language learning could be the oral story, the conversation, the performed routine.

A question often put to the subscribers of whole language, which is equally pertinent to this approach of situated pragmatics, has to with how a child can learn the parts if the parts are not taught. One response has been that children will deduce the parts from the whole by realizing the regularities on repeated exposures. That is to say, they will treat wholes as comprised of slots, and will understand structure by classifying together the elements that fit particular slots (see Nelson, 1991a, 1991b). Slot-filling, then becomes one view of how children move from the gestalt understandings to understanding elements within the gestalt. It is an answer that proponents of whole language as well as situated pragmatics might give to the subscribers of a traditional analytic and skills-based approach to language teaching. (See Norris and Hoffman, 1993a and 1993b, for a discussion of syntactic "parsing" as a way to move from whole understandings to understanding constituent parts.)

The view of learning as a processing of filling in elements in appropriate slots has long been around. Structured language programs of the 1950s, for example, presented children with chains of words and required them to fill in elements in their appropriate place in the chain. Grammar was seen as a slot-filling enterprise wherein words that fit into the same place in a grammatical construction were seen as understood as a particular part of speech. Nouns followed verbs and articles, verbs are following by aspectual markers (-ing) or tense markers (-ed, -en).

Pragmatic approaches to language intervention have also made liberal use of notions of "slot filling" as a strategy to help children understand structured relations between elements in a grammatical, event, or discourse frame. For example, Nelson (1985, 1986, 1991a, 1991b) has suggested that children first learn basic conceptual relations of items such as foods, social roles, or object identities by observing which elements can be substituted for one another in a given slot in a familiar event. Foods are things that can be eaten during mealtimes, caretakers are people who give baths during bathtime, balls are objects that can be rolled and thrown in a ball playing event.

Similarly, Bruner's notion of event scaffolding as a learning context includes in it an understanding of how elements fill slots in the whole. The adult at first provides a schema with all elements contained in it, and later invites the child to fill in the relevant components by providing the openings in the frame for the child to complete (Ratner & Bruner, 1978; Wood, Bruner, & Ross, 1976). Those who have discussed scaffolding as a teaching strategy (e.g., Cazden, 1988, pp. 104–110; Kirchner, 1991a) portray language learning as a process of knowing what elements go in the identified places in a discourse or event schema. For some schemas, the slots are located in action sequences (e.g., saying peek-a-boo when the blanket is removed); for others they are located in discourse sequences (e.g., learning what to say during the telling of a story; answering a question when the response slot needs filling). Kirchner (1991a) described the process as "using 'substitution' and 'replacement' strategies which hold the predictable frame and meaning constant, while varying the constituent parts" (p. 321).

Besides knowing where elements fit into the whole, children learning through whole language and situated pragmatic approaches will need to know how to make sense of the elements in relation to the overall structure. There is some evidence that children can successfully understand what elements go where in an event, without understanding why. The box on the next page is a transcript of an exchange between a teacher and Robbie, a 9-year-old child with autism. The two had been working with the Distar program in which teachers provide answers to questions, along with the question. Robbie developed a "right answer" strategy by filling in the slot requiring an answer with the statement accompanying the question. But, as one can tell from his error, he did not always understand the meaning relations between the questions and the answers.

The bold phrases provided by the teacher gave the child the discourse support for arriving at an answer to the question asked of him. The prob-

Adult:	What is this?
Robbie:	(no answer)
Adult:	**A napkin.** What is this, Robbie?
Robbie:	**A napkin.**
Adult:	What do we do with a napkin?
Robbie:	We play . . .
Adult:	We wipe our mouth with a napkin. **Wipe our mouth?**
Robbie:	**Wipe our mouth?**
Adult:	**And hand?**
Robbie:	**And hand?**
Adult:	Wipe our mouth and our hand, **when we eat.** What do we do with a napkin?
Robbie:	**When we eat.**
	(Duchan, 1983, p. 56)

lem with the exercise is that the child is able to respond correctly to the question without fully understanding what is being asked of him. As is revealed from his answer "when we eat," he might be responding rotely, failing to use the meaning carried in the discourse to figure out his answer.

Robbie's clever error in the last line illustrates the danger of relying too heavily on slot-filling strategies of teaching. One needs to go beyond slot-filling when scaffolding children's discourse to help them understand what is going on. Learners using whole language and situated pragmatic approaches must understand not only which constituents are candidates for slot replacement, but also the social, cultural, and meaning significance of the frame so as to select elements that best fit its slots.

■□ SUMMARY

This chapter has compared situated pragmatics with other approaches to language intervention. The companion approach to situated pragmatics in the area of reading is called whole language. Other interventions which served as the focus for this chapter were based in behaviorism, derived from linguistic theory and analyses, cognitive approaches, infor-mation processing approaches, and approaches that are pragmatic in fo-cus, but abstracted from the immediate context. The argument made by situated pragmatics is that approaches that involve altering the input to children in the name of making something simpler may be misconceived because such alterations involve a context change, which may diminish children's access to contextual cues needed to make sense of what is going on.

Situated Pragmatics: Approaches for Children with Various Communicative Needs

The approach to intervention put forward in this book has been one of finding ways to support children so that they can come to understand and participate readily in their everyday life experiences. The aim of the book has been to develop and present ideas behind situated pragmatics as well as to outline the contents of six different support contexts. The focus has been to broaden our current approaches to language intervention, to include more of what is going on in the situation, and to change our view from an abstract notion of pragmatics to one that is situated in the concrete circumstances of particular occasions.

So far we have not discussed how the situated approach might be implemented to meet specific needs of particular learners in the unique circumstances of their everyday lives. In this last chapter, an effort will be made to discuss what a situated pragmatics approach might consist of for particular children in specific contexts and how the approach can be tailored to meet the different everyday needs of those children.

■□ TAILORING SITUATED PRAGMATICS TO MEET SPECIFIC NEEDS

Subscribing to a situated view of pragmatics is likely to change what clinicians think and what they aim for in designing goals for children. It is also likely to substantially alter how its subscribers conduct interventions. It is apparent from what has gone before in this book that support can be provided in a wide variety of ways. The method leaves the followers of this approach with many decisions to make. In what contexts should the support be provided? Who should provide the support? What types of support should be provided for particular children? How might targeted support relate to targeted goals? What specific methods could be used to provide support for a child?

In What Situational Contexts Should the Support Be Provided?

The support provider who carries out an effective situated pragmatics approach will need to join children in locations they frequent: at home, at school, or in the community. In these sites clinicians may themselves support a child, or better yet, the clinician may be able to alter contexts so that support is provided automatically by those in the targeted context who interact with the children. This automatic support is the ultimate goal, because the approach's success rests on the premise that support be provided a child throughout the day — a feat impossible for any one person.

Particular support contexts, like particular intervention goals, will need to be identified so that the support providers can keep track of what they are doing. Providers may target contexts that are most accessible or most amenable to change. Or they might focus on contexts most in need of change.

An examination of what the child does everyday would yield a variety of possible choices. One can, for example, assess how the child performs in different contexts throughout the day. Such an assessment might be carried out by using a questionnaire, by conducting an interview with those who are in the child's life, or by observing the child directly. A first step would be to determine what the child does in different locales at school (cafeteria, playground, classroom), at home (kitchen, playroom, on the porch), or in the community (zoo, stores, restaurants). Targeted contexts can be selected based on who, among the child's affiliates, is most likely to provide support or what contexts are most in need of change. Or they may be selected according to what type of support the child needs.

One focus of the assessment would be to identify contexts in which the child has difficulty. The child may, on some occasions, refuse to participate, show signs of stress or frustration, or be unable to perform successfully. If a child does not feel successful in, say, a reading group in third grade, the supporter may design a reading context in which the child's performance is not explicitly evaluated, such as the face saving contexts described by Eriks-Brophy and Crago (1993) (see Chapter 3).

Successful contexts also need to be identified. Occasions when children perform competently can be used to support them in contexts where they have difficulty. Children who are successful in, for example, a kindergarten activity involving storytelling could be supported in other areas of communication by transforming the trouble areas into a storytelling event. The kindergarten teacher, Vivian Paley (1990), used storytelling with a child who did not engage readily in the activities of her kindergarten classroom. Jason "speaks only of helicopters and broken blades, and he appears indifferent to the play and stories that surround him" (Paley, 1990, p. 11). Jason's helicopter became the transition object that allowed him to enter the play of the other children. (See the box below for an example of Paley's support.)

Supporting Social Interaction Between Kindergarten Children Through Storytelling and Story Enactment

Paley: You turned off your motor when Simon told you to land. Now you know all about stories. Do you want to tell one?

Jason: Yes. And a helicopter. A turbo prop. It's flying.

(In the story room, Jason zooms around the rug as I read his story, continuing to fly several moments beyond the last words on the page. When he stops, I say:)

Paley: I wonder if the helicopter sees another plane?

Jason: Someone

Paley: Which someone?

Jason: The squirrel someone.

(continued)

Simon:	He means me! I'm the plane, right?
Jason:	(nods)
	(Simon imitates the helicopter roar we have come to know so well. Chins forward, arms in motion, the boys fly together in formation.)

Who Should Provide the Support?

Support providers would best be selected from those the child spends time with in the contexts targeted for change. Although traditional roles for our profession have dictated that speech-language pathologists (SLPs) work directly with children in speech rooms or clinics, this model of service delivery does not meet the needs identified in situated pragmatics of being with the child in the child's world. However, new models more in keeping with the requirements of situated pragmatics have emerged in recent years. SLPs now act as consultants to parents or other professionals with the aim of designing techniques and programs for enhancing the communication of particular children. In addition, school SLPs have been directly engaged with children in their classrooms, rather than in the speech room (Miller, 1989; Nelson, 1989; Norris, 1989). Finally, collaborative consultation teams have become commonplace (Harris, 1990; Idol, Paolucci-Whitcomb, & Nevin, 1986). Teams of teachers, parents, physical and occupational therapists, and speech-language pathologists work together to create plans for children with disabilities; and all those involved in the planning also work together to carry out and evaluate their plans.

Because the aim is to provide support for children in their everyday lives, it becomes crucial to involve individuals who interact with the child on a daily basis in the support plan. Thus the SLP when using the collaborative, consulting, and teaming approaches serves to (1) organize and work with teams to design the communicative support system for individuals; (2) work with others to create an individualized educational plan, a family plan, or a personal futures plan for supporting a child; (3) consult with individuals who are carrying out the support to fine tune the support to meet the child's needs; (4) evaluate contexts to determine the key support people and what support they can best provide; and (5) work with others to discover competencies in individuals and to alter everyday interactive contexts to build upon those competencies.

What Type of Support Should Be Provided for Particular Children?

Situated pragmatics requires that meaningful and positive support that fits a child's everyday needs be provided. The six support contexts outlined in this book can be used as a guide for thinking about the child's needs. Supports may be tailored to fit what are seen as the child's difficulties or they may be designed to build on the child's strengths. Emotional support, for example, may be provided for children who frequently display a lack of self-esteem. Or emotional support can provide an otherwise secure child with the confidence and encouragement to explore an area that he or she finds intimidating.

The types of support contexts, although treated separately in this book, can be administered together and even at the same time. Contexts designed to enhance children's learning include a variety of simultaneously offered supports. A story context used for learning a language structure, for example, is likely to provide the child opportunities for social support (for experiencing different roles, interacting with peers), emotional support (for providing social referencing, affect attunement), functional support (for understanding how plots serve to motivate characters' actions), physical support (for using pictures to guide one's thinking and pages in a book to create suspense), and discourse support (for reading the text and coming to understand the discourse of a story).

Situated pragmatics calls for different types of support to be provided on the same occasion. It also calls for designing different occasions to meet a child's particular needs. We are familiar with techniques designed to elicit particular structures from children — and have called them elicitation procedures (e.g., Lund & Duchan, 1993). Similarly, contexts can be designed to offer children different types of support. For example, different discourse genres provide unique opportunities for supporting learning, and different events promote different learning opportunities. For these reasons, it can be useful to choose contexts to fit identified goals and afford the optimum support to help a child achieve those goals.

Sonnenmeier (1994) illustrates this concept of event affordances in her discussion of how to support role learning in preschool children. She shows, for instance, how a camping activity allows for different actors to carry out activities together with little regard for role. Anyone might participate in cooking, washing up after eating, or creating a campfire. Other events such as playing house may require more obvious and inflexible role-related activities. If the intervention goal is understanding or expanding roles, it behooves the support provider to target events that emphasize role relations.

How Do Targeted Supports
Relate to Targeted Goals?

Support contexts offer a means for achieving goals yet they need not be directly related to goal statements. A child may have goals that involve learning conversational discourse. The targeted supports for achieving conversational goals should include opportunities for creating recriprocal roles. For example, it would be useful to create a social arrangement that is egalitarian, in which test questions are minimized and real questions are prevalent. It would also help to create role relations having to do with who has knowledge about the topic being discussed. In the most authentic conversations the targeted child should convey information unknown to others. The task at hand thus would involve having others find out something new from the child through the course of a conversation with him.

Targeted support could also involve emotional support, encouraging children so that they can proceed with confidence. Such support may involve priming the child about what is about to take place, creating a context in which the child actually wants to convey information to a partner, and providing the child with a nonjudgmental context for exploring ways to carry out conversations. In the following example, Wally, provides his classmate Rose with conversational support, and does so, according to their teacher Vivian Paley, throughout the school day.

Wally and Rose

Rose watched Wally's moods, but Wally listened to Rose's words. To be exact, Wally examined what was wrong with Rose's words. Too often, Rose did not "make sense." Her reasoning could be hard to follow, and she lacked the flexibility to clarify her statements.

Lisa: 1 (Pouring tea.) My daddy says black people come from Africa.

Wally: 2 I come from Chicago.

Lisa: 3 White people are born in America.

Wally: 4 I'm black and I was born in Chicago.

Rose: 5 Because more people come dressed up like they want to.

Wally: 6 How do they dress up?

Rose:	7	You know, like going to church or someplace.
Wally:	8	You mean if they're black?
Rose:	9	They can dress up like they want to.
Wally:	10	I see what she means.
	11	Like getting dressed up to go to church?
Rose:	12	Like they want to.
Wally:	13	Not in a black dress, right?
	14	You can wear a white dress?
Rose:	15	Yes.

(from Paley, 1981, p. 47)

A third type of support that is likely to be essential in developing a child's conversational abilities is **discourse support**. For example, ideas related to the topic can be rehearsed beforehand and called on when needed, scaffolding might be done to relate apparently tangential comments to the main topic, or feedback can be provided if the child does not observe turn-taking conventions.

What Specific Methods Could Be Used in Providing Support for a Child?

The methods discussed in this book have been far ranging, including not only how one might talk to and with children about what is happening, but also how one might alter roles, emotional content, emotional response, physical aspects of the situation, and the activities that are going on. Specific methods in a situated approach will depend on what is going on in the situation, who the interactants are, the child's needs in that context, and the supporter's goals for the child in that situation. The best methods are those that allow the child to make sense of what is going on and provide an emotionally safe environment so that the child can participate willingly and meaningfully. Examples of some techniques that can be used in the six support contexts for children at different stages in their development are listed in Table 9–1, along with references for further reading. Most are already among the established methods used by clinicians, teachers, parents, and peers. Some are not. What ties them to situated pragmatics is that they can be carried out and tailored to any child's real-life experiences.

TABLE 9-1

Examples of Specific Techniques for Providing Different Types of Contextual Support for Children with Differing Needs.

Context	Techniques
Social Context	Supporting children's role learning.
Early learner:	Enact scripts involving family roles (father, mother, siblings), teacher-student roles, community roles (grocer-customer, waiter-customer, doctor-patient)
Mature learner:	Enact scripts involving employer-job applicant, partners on a date, conversational partners, talk show hosts-guests (Donahue, 1984).
Emotional context	Responding to the child's emotional state.
Early learner:	Respond in kind to the rhythm and content of child's moods and actions (Stern, 1985); use events in stories to develop understanding of emotion in self and others (Paley, 1990).
Mature learner:	Provide emotional support (coaching) when child experiences frustration or difficulty; change interactive style of teacher to create classrooms that are more like those of the Inuit in which children who are having difficulty can maintain face (Eriks-Brophy & Crago, 1993).
Functional context	Helping the child communicate and act on his own goals and those of others.
Early learner:	Design events that the child is excited about and ways that a child can request the events and request items within the event (e.g., the sequence boxes in Stillman & Battle, 1984).
Mature learner:	Use stories to interpret motivations of others to the child so as to help him or her develop a sense of others' agendas (Hewitt, 1994); have children write their own stories or talk about events with plots involving evaluation by characters, or deception and mystery (Hewitt & Duchan, in press).
Physical context	Encouraging social interaction in ongoing events and the ability to describe past events.

Context	Techniques
Physical contexts *(continued)*	
Early learner:	Create alternative spaces in the classroom that children can manipulate and where they can practice life-related interactions through play (Educational Productions, 1988).
Mature learner:	Provide communicative support at afterschool programs where children are able to socialize informally during a physically based recreational goal (e.g., weaving, pottery, cooking, ball games) (Hood, McDermott, & Cole, 1980); use snapshots and objects from home to support reporting of past events (Brinton & Fujiki, 1994).
Event Context	Supporting participation in everyday events
Early learner:	Develop joint interaction routines between teacher and child, parent and child, and peers and child that occur throughout the day and carry out meaningful functions (Snyder-McLean, Solomonson, McLean, & Sack, 1984).
Mature learner:	Discuss or create written scripts with the child to help the child understand and participate in complex or rule-based events (Shultz, 1979); provide social support such as peer coaches to maintain face during events where knowledge is insufficient (Hood, McDermott, & Cole, 1980).
Discourse context	Fostering event descriptions
Early learner:	Create occasions in which the child has opportunities to tell about an emotional event in the past (Miller & Sperry, 1988); scaffold answers to questions about past events using a notebook that goes between home and school (Lund & Duchan, 1987).
Mature learner:	Tell children about significant happenings and ask whether anything like that ever happened to them (Peterson & McCabe, 1983).

■□ SITUATED PRAGMATICS FOR CHILDREN WITH DIFFERENT LANGUAGE LEARNING NEEDS

Previous chapters focused on the nature of support contexts for helping children learn to communicate and paid little heed to how these approaches might be used to promote learning in particular targeted areas. How might such an approach be used to help children develop their vocabulary, help children express targeted speech acts, or understand particular grammatical structures? We now consider ways that advocates of situated pragmatics might attain such goals. We will also discuss how situated pragmatics approaches might be tailored to children of different ages, levels of ability, and types of disability.

Having and Using Words

Vocabulary is often a target of therapy for children at various stages of their language learning. Vocabulary intervention programs are sometimes designed and used to teach children their first words. Children who are candidates for such programs are those who are moving from preverbal to verbal stages of language development. A situated pragmatics approach, rather than treating words as vocabulary, would treat words as tools that can serve to reference ideas and to make sense of what is going on. The focus in the situated framework would be to choose a domain of interest to the child and build a lexicon of related ideas to aid him or her in sensemaking. Vocabulary goals would be cast as functional for the child and taught as a related set in the context of an everyday event. (See Brinton and Fujiki [1994] for ways conversational discourse can be used to achieve vocabulary goals.)

   Another approach to vocabulary teaching that is consistent with situated pragmatics is the organic reading method developed by Sylvia Ashton-Warner (1963). She allowed children to select words that were precious to them, and offered them cards with the word written on them to take home, thereby supporting their learning by drawing on the children's sense of what is important to them.

Teaching to Children's Understandings: A Sensemaking Approach

I hear that in other infant rooms widespread illustration is used to introduce the reading vocabulary to a five-year-

> old, a vocabulary chosen by adult educationists. I use pictures, too, to introduce the reading vocabulary, but they are pictures of the inner vision and the captions are chosen by the children themselves. True, the picture of the outer, adult-chosen pictures can be meaningful and delightful to children; but it is the captions of the mind pictures that have the power and the light. For whereas the illustrations perceived by the outer eye cannot be other than interesting, the illustrations seen by the inner eye are organic, and it is the captioning of these that I call the "Key Vocabulary".
>
> (Ashton-Warner, 1963, p. 32)

Ashton-Warner let the children choose the words that were to be part of their reading and writing vocabulary. Another approach is for the clinician or teacher to pick the words and to base the selection on what words are needed to accomplish certain purposes or achieve certain types of sensemaking. (See the following box for an example of this situated approach outlined by Crystal, 1987.)

> **A Situated Approach to Vocabulary Learning**
>
> First of all, it is important to choose words which have some motivation for the child — where there is some reasonable change that the word will relate to aspects of the child's life.
>
> The point to be appreciated is that the words for different facial parts are not equivalent in their pragmatic force. "Nose" becomes particularly important when the child has a cold, and has to keep wiping it. "Teeth" are important at certain times of the day, when they have to be brushed. "Eyes" are important when something gets into them, or when people point out the different colours.
>
> (Crystal, 1987, p. 51)

Overall, the situated pragmatics approach regards vocabulary learning as situated knowledge. Children with too few words would be thought of as needing support in expressing, through words, their communicative intents or their favorite things, and as needing help to better participate in the events and discourse of their everyday lives.

Encouraging Single-act Intents

A number of language programs have been designed to teach children particular intents, such as requests (Olswang, Kriegsmann, & Master-george, 1982) or topic initiations (Brinton & Fujiki, 1994). Elicitation of different intents has been carried out in a variety of contexts so that children come to learn that requests, for example, can occur in many situations. Generalization is often considered as the final test of whether the intervention worked (Leonard, 1981).

Busy children going about their own purposes need many speech acts to have choices in their social interactions. There is some evidence that the more situated approaches are more successful in helping children learn to understand and use speech acts. For example, Calculator (1988) compared a child's success with two intervention approaches, one using a nonsituated picture selection task and a second using a situated task. When an an 8-year-old nonspeaking child was asked to look at the object the teacher named, he was unable to do so after 2 years of training. However, when the child's choice of objects related to a request for something meaningful in his life, he was able to consistently choose between items after 6 months of training (looking at the chosen location for taking a nap; looking at a desired snack from a group of snacks, etc.). (For more on the situated approach to intentionality, see Chapter 3.)

A situated approach to single-act intents would elicit and model expressions of targeted intents in keeping with richly textured event, discourse, or affective contexts. The approach would aim to support the child in his efforts to get what he wants in particular contexts. It thus differs from an abstract pragmatics approach that is designed to help a child to, say, request things in general.

Also evolving from a situated view is the idea that children's expressions of intents have a broader scope than single-act intents. Requests, cast as single acts, focus on isolated utterances. Requests, seen as part of agendas, focus on multiple acts, both verbal and nonverbal, that are needed to accomplish certain goals. For example, in situated pragmatics a child might be provided with support to work with another child to get an object out of reach. The series of acts and accompanying talk to figure out what to do to achieve the goal are all means to accomplish an agenda and can be construed as part of training to accomplish goals that offer children more alternatives than do single-act requests.

Supporting Grammatical Learning

A situated pragmatics approach for children who are found to have grammatical differences would first ask how the structural differences exhibited by a child fit with the child's situational understandings. The child's misuse of the past tense may come from an understanding that the past tense indicates that events have finished rather than that events occurred sometime in the past (see Weist, Wysocka, Witkowska-Stadnik, Buczowska, & Konieczna, 1984, for a discussion of this "deficit tense hypothesis"). If children have unconventional understandings of grammatical forms, a situated approach could help them realize and repair their misunderstandings.

When children's language difficulties are primarily structural in nature, a situated pragmatics intervention might still be warranted, so that children can acquire the new forms in a sensible and everyday context. A nice example of naturally occurring learning of complex syntax is provided in Skarakis-Doyle and Mentis (1991). These authors describe a child who added a clause to a previous adult utterance to create compound and complex sentences (e.g., *Adult:* Oh, they had sheep there. *Child:* And they ran around.) Thus, although the adult was not aware of it, she was providing the needed discourse support for the child to build complex sentences.

The child in the Skarakis-Doyle and Mentis (1991) study who created his own learning context — a context that was outside of the awareness of his interlocutor — offers us both encouragement and a method for providing a naturally occurring discourse supportive context to help children learn complex syntax. Indeed, there is some evidence from the literature that this is an important avenue for learning and a natural way of applying the situated pragmatics approach to teaching syntax (Culatta, 1984; Scherer & Olswang, 1984, 1989).

The discourse support for learning syntax presented in the above studies (Scherer & Olswang, 1984, 1989; Skarakis-Doyle & Mentis, 1991) was offered in the children's first language. Schieffelin (1994) provides an interesting extension of this procedure in her description of how Haitian children are provided support for learning English as a second language. Adult speakers of Haitian Kreyol and English talked to the children in their first language providing them with support for learning English. Schieffelin (1994) argues convincingly from this that discourse support involving code shifting from the first language to the second can facilitate learning of the second language.

Therefore, a situated approach to intervention aimed at improving a child's language structure would look for the pragmatic impact of the targeted structure and, where possible, design functional communicative contexts that highlight the importance of that structure. Discourse support to promote grammatical learning can thus be provided in naturally occurring contexts.

▪️□ SITUATED PRAGMATICS AS APPLIED TO CHILDREN WITH DIFFERENT DIAGNOSTIC CLASSIFICATIONS

With the wide variety of intervention approaches and the possibilities in each, how does a clinician pick an appropriate method to meet the needs of children with different disabilities? The framework argued for in this book leads to the conclusion that intervention approaches are most likely to work best when they are based on what children can do in contexts of everyday life. This philosophical approach supersedes approaches designed to fit a child's general diagnosis. That is to say, a situated approach for working with a child with echolalia should vary with the child and should not be dedicated only to those with autism, even though that is the group most often associated with the "symptom" of echolalia. Rather, support would differ for the particular echo and the occasion it was used (Duchan, 1994b; Kirchner, 1991b). The approach, then, can be said to be blind to the child's overall diagnosis.

▪️□ SITUATED PRAGMATICS AS APPLIED TO CHILDREN OF DIFFERENT DEVELOPMENTAL ABILITIES

Clinicians working in a situated pragmatics framework will need to rely on the context to design intervention programs. In so doing, they would depend less heavily on what is known about developmental stages of typical children. The rationale for placing less emphasis on normative information is that children of different ages and stages in development may need similar support contexts to help them participate in their life contexts. Further, children of the same age and stage whose lives present different challenges will require different support contexts. The goals using a situated approach will depend on what particular children need to make better sense of their worlds and what they need to communicate better with others. The approach thus questions the desirability of using developmental sequences as primary guidelines for establishing intervention goals.

Normatively based programs rest on the assumption that children, whatever their abilities, progress through the same learning stages (Johnston, 1985). This developmental assumption gives rise to programs whose serial progression is predetermined and normative (see Table 9–2 for examples of language intervention programs based on the developmental model).

TABLE 9-2
Developmentally Focused Language Programs.

Language Development

Vocabulary programs (Gillham, 1979)

Development of semantic relations (Lahey, 1988; Miller & Yoder, 1974)

Developmental syntax programs (Lee, Koenigsknecht, & Mulhern, 1975)

Cognitive Development

From context bound to decontextualized learning (Norris & Hoffman, 1993a)

From perceptual to conceptual levels (Blank, 1983; Blank, Rose, & Berlin, 1978)

Through the sensorimotor stages (Lahey, 1988, pp. 203-207)

A developmental approach may or may not be sensitive to a particular child's unique understandings and learning abilities. There is some evidence to indicate that some children with communication disorders do fit "the normative pattern" (Gillham, 1990). In these cases, programs that organize the presentation of information in accord with normally developing children may be beneficial, provided the information is in keeping with the child's understandings of what is going on.

There are indicators that some children learn differently from typical children and do not fall into the developmental patterns expected for their language age-mates (for a review, see Reed, 1994). For these children a nondevelopmental approach needs to be designed to meet their communication needs.

Still other evidence shows that even typical children may fall outside of what is thought to be the normal pattern of development (Ferguson, 1979; Fillmore, 1989; Peters, 1983). For example, some children do not choose the analytic approach to language learning presumed by the normative literature, and instead select larger units as an entry into the language system (Duchan, 1994b; Pine & Lieven, 1993). An emerging literature on individual differences among typical children would argue for individually designed programs and would challenge clinicians' undue reliance on developmental norms to guide their intervention approaches.

To summarize, a language interventionist needs to ask whether the stages of development observed for normal children are relevant for particular children with language learning problems. There may be reasons why a child skips a stage, or shows advanced abilities in one domain and difficulties in another. (See the following for a striking example of how a developmental approach might be misapplied.)

An Example of How Readiness Is Misapplied

This is a true life experience of a mother of a child with cerebral palsy (as conveyed by Barbara Hoskins, a speech language pathologist). The school personnel, following a strictly developmental model, told this mother that her son was not close to being ready to work on reading in his special classroom, because dressing came earlier in the developmental sequence and he could not yet dress himself. The mother realized her son was unable to dress himself because of his motor problems, and that he had special difficulty zipping his pants. Hoskins suggested that she buy her son Velcro™ pants, and thereby solve the readiness problem.

(Paraphrased from Nelson, 1993, p. 11)

The readiness problem demonstrates the developmental fallacy inherent in traditional approaches to language intervention. Just because typical development shows stage-like progressions, there is no reason to believe that these stages are inherently related and required for learning. Crawling may be achieved before walking for many children, but may not be a necessary precursor for walking in either typical or atypical learners. What does make sense for intervention is to sequence learnings in which one stage is foundational for another. This takes us back to the sensemaking point. A strict developmental approach would say a child has learned to zip up his pants before learning to read, because that's the sequence of normal learning. Velcro-type solutions are important remedies, but they wouldn't be needed if the developmental approach was tied to the approach advocated in situational pragmatics.

■□ SEQUENTIAL PROGRESSION OF PROGRAMMING IN A SITUATED PRAGMATICS APPROACH

There exists a notion among clinicians that beginning learners require more structure in teaching than those who are more advanced. Highly structured activities often are recommended for children at first, and more allowances made later. For example, programs designed to help children learn to communicate using facilitated communication, begin with controlled activities (called "set work") and progress to more open-ended conversation (Biklen, 1990; Crossley & McDonald, 1980; Schubert, 1992). Indeed, there is a literature supporting this notion. Less advanced children in some studies have been shown to benefit more from didactic approaches than those who were more advanced (e.g., Friedman & Friedman, 1980).

But for every study that favors more structure for beginning learners, one can find another study, that shows the opposite. Some studies show that less advanced children learn more from child-centered and less structured intervention than they do from more didactic intervention (e.g., Norris & Hoffman, 1990; Yoder, Kaiser, & Alpert, 1991). Others show that older children benefit more from more structured approaches than from less structured approaches (e.g., Yoder, Kaiser, & Alpert, 1991). And still others that show that older, more advanced language learners do better with child-centered, less structured approaches than they do with more structured approaches (e.g., Friedman & Friedman, 1980). Lastly, there are studies that show no differences between the didactic and child-centered approaches for children whatever their ages or language abilities (Cole & Dale, 1986).

The varied results present a dilemma for the clinician who needs to select a specific method for a particular child. The recommendation from the situated pragmatics philosophy would be to change the domain of choices. That is to say, rather than seeing the relevant domain as the amount of structure, the clinician who is based in the situated pragmatics philosophy may choose the method based on how well the child makes sense of what is being presented. A highly structured activity that is relevant, exciting, and meaningful to the child is preferable to a structured activity that is uninteresting. An unstructured activity that contains elements which allow the child to receive the needed support for learning is preferred over a structured one (or unstructured one) that is less tied to the child's understandings. The amount of structure, then, becomes secondary to the sensemaking effort.

■ PLANNING SUPPORT CONTEXTS AND EVALUATING PROGRESS OF SELECTED CHILDREN

The approach of situated pragmatics requires a broad support plan that includes the following choices: (1) selection of children to receive services; (2) determination of communicative abilities and needs of selected children; (3) targeting of communicative goals; (4) identification of support contexts for providing services to selected children in light of targeted goals; (5) selection of support providers for different targeted support contexts; (6) tracking children's performance under different conditions of support. Figure 9–1 outlines these issues and offers a format for creating a support plan to meet the needs of individual children.

■◻ CAUTIONS

This method of situated support, like other methods, contains within it opportunities for misuse. There are times when a provider may misconstrue a child's needs and provide either too much or too little support. The aim of a supporter is the same as Goldilocks' was — to determine the situation that is "just right." Wally, in the example provided earlier in this chapter, provided his friend Rose with the bridges needed to relate her thoughts to the ongoing topic of conversation. He did not speak for her, but instead was apparently successful at making Rose's communicative efforts meaningful to all participating in the conversation. But what if Rose did not mean what Wally thought she did? In that case, Wally may have been putting unwanted words in Rose's mouth. Such occasions are contexts in which intended support may have an opposite effect — a lack of support.

Every approach should therefore be accompanied by checks to guard against misuse. Table 9–3 offers a list of cautions and ways to keep in check the efforts of the enthusiast who adopts a situated pragmatics approach while failing to appreciate the need to fit the methods to the needs of the child and the demands of the context.

■◻ SUMMARY

In this chapter we answered some specific questions that might be posed in carrying out the situated pragmatics approach. We also discussed how a situated pragmatics approach might be applied to a variety of the targeted goals. When applied to vocabulary teaching, teaching language structure, and teaching single-act intents, the approach leads the clinician to change the way he or she thinks of those goals. Vocabulary instruction becomes a matter of helping children have access to full participation in identified situations; morphology and syntax training are associated with intentionality and achieving agendas.

Child's name _____

Child's Age _____ DOB _____

Date of report _____

Communication competencies of child: _____

_____

_____

Communication goals for child: _____

_____

_____

Contexts targeted for support: _____

_____

_____

Targeted support providers: _____

_____

_____

Means for tracking support effectiveness: _____

_____

_____

Means for tracking child's communicative progress: _____

_____

_____

_____

FIGURE 9-1
A plan for supporting children's communication in contexts of everyday life.

TABLE 9-3
Cautions and Checks to Guard Against Misuse of the Situated Pragmatics Approach to Supporting Children's Communication.

Cautions

Provision of too little support

Children who are provided too little support may show it by resorting to rote learning of scaffolded material and fail to make sense of information being provided.

Provision of too much support

Children may feel their intents or agendas are being co-opted, or taken in a direction they do not want to go. This is described in the literature on facilitated communication as too much influence or as an issue of authorship (for a summary see Duchan, 1993b).

Provision of the wrong sort of support

Children's difficulties may be misconstrued. For example, they may be thought to be unmotivated to talk and may be given emotional support when their problems are actually physically based.

Creation of support dependencies

Children may come to rely on supported contexts and in so doing may fail to develop or communicate outside supported contexts.

Checks

Examine changes in performance over time

Contexts that are supportive are more likely to result in related changes in children's performance either within a supported session or across many sessions. Conditions that do not result in changes may be ones that are not attuned to the child's needs.

Encourage the child to protest unwanted support

Children should be asked frequently if the provided support is appropriate to their needs. Questions such as "is that what you meant?" or "right?" can be asked, and ways offered for the child to protest a type of support or to correct the provider on specific incorrect interpretations.

Monitor the support given

The support provider should vary the degree of support given to gauge whether the support is "just right." Some contexts, such as those containing stress, may require more support than others.

An argument was made against selecting an intervention approach to fit a child's diagnosis, or even to fit a child's deficit pattern or developmental stage. Rather, the situated pragmatics approach would select goals and procedures based on the children's aims and needs as they are played out in their everyday lives. The chapter ended with an outline of the decisions that were made when planning support contexts and a set of cautions for guarding against the possible abuses arising from the methods.

Thus this book ends as well as this chapter. Accompanying the content in these pages is the hope and invitation that the situated pragmatics approach will be added to or substituted for other approaches designed to support children as they engage in the difficult and rewarding process of living their lives through communication.

Epilogue

I It is the year 2030, and two young adults meet for the first time. As they begin talking, they realize that they attended the same elementary school in Chicago, Illinois and, even more coincidentally, they were in the same kindergarten class. They remember it vividly, because their teacher, Vivian Paley, taught them not only how to get along with each other, but how to support one another to accomplish the stories and other activities that took place during the day (see Paley, 1990, for a detailed description of her approach).

Jason: I don't believe it! You were the one who acted out my stories and who gave me such support whenever I needed it. Remember when all I wanted to do was to be a helicopter? That was amazing to me when other kids invited me, in my helicopter mode, to join in on what they were doing. Those were my favorite times in kinderagrten.

Katie: Yes. You were the most exciting kid in the class. We were all flattered when you would pay attention to us, and we loved acting out stories. But you sure could make us mad. You were too noisy for me, and we hated it when you messed up our activities.

Jason: Sorry about that. But thanks for hanging in there with me. I had a hard time transitioning from that class. My first grade teacher wanted me to sit in one place and do what the rest of the class was doing. She drove me nuts! I was always being punished. I spent my entire first grade in time-out. I wouldn't have been able to make it through primary grades if I had had to put up with one more day of that.

Katie: What happened after that?

Jason: I got placed in classes with cooperative groups. They were much easier to deal with. They allowed me to move around and to learn at my own pace. I also loved math, and was able to help the other kids in math, and they helped me in reading. I did fine from then on. I even gave up my helicopter persona and settled down some. What about you?

Katie: I grew up and went to college. I became a teacher in Chicago Public Schools. I am working with three or four kids who are having a hard time with school, and I am looking for ways to do for them what Vivian Paley did for us. It's a lot of fun — and a lot of work. And you?

Jason: I'm in tourism. I joined a small company located in Niagara Falls, New York and am a part-owner now. My main job is to take our customers for a joy ride above the falls. I've been doing that for 3 years now, ever since I became a helicopter pilot.

References

Ashton-Warner, S. (1963). *Teacher.* New York: Simon & Schuster.

Au, K. (1980). Participation structures in a reading lesson with Hawaiian children: Analysis of a culturally appropriate instructional event. *Anthropology and Education Quarterly, 11,* 91–115.

Austin, J. (1962). *How to do things with words.* Oxford, NJ: Oxford University Press.

Ayer, A. J. (1964). *Language, truth and logic* (2nd ed.). New York: Dover Books. (First published in 1934)

Baer, D., & Guess, D. (1973). Teaching productive noun suffixes to severely retarded children. *American Journal of Mental Deficiency, 77,* 498–505.

Bakhtin, M. (1981). *The dialogic imagination: Four essays by M. M. Bahktin.* (M. Holquist, Ed). Austin: University of Texas Press.

Bakhtin, M. (1986). Speech genres and other late essays. (C. Emerson & M. Holquist, Eds.; V. McGee, Trans). Austin: University of Texas Press.

Bartlett, F. (1932). *Remembering: A study in experimental and social psychology.* New York: Cambridge University Press.

Barton, A. (1970a). Soft boxes in hard schools. In S. Repo (Ed.), *This book is about schools* (pp. 195–208). New York: Vintage Books.

Barton, A. (1970b). The hard-soft school. In S. Repo (Ed.), *This book is about schools* (pp. 183–194). New York: Vintage Books.

Bates, E., Benigini, T., Bretherton, I., Camaioni, G., & Volterra, V. (1979). *The emergence of symbols: Cognition and communication in infancy.* New York: Academic Press.

Bates, E., & MacWhinney, B. (1987). Competition, variation, and language learning. In B. MacWhinney (Ed.), *Mechanisms of language acquisition* (pp. 157–193). Hillsdale, NJ: Lawrence Erlbaum.

Bauman, R., & Sherzer, J. (1989). *Explorations in the ethnography of speaking* (2nd ed.). New York: Cambridge University Press.

Becker L., & Silverstein, J. (1984). Clinician-child discourse: A replication study. *Journal of Speech and Hearing Disorders, 49,* 104–106.

Bedrosian, J. (1985). An approach to developing conversational competence. In D. Ripich & F. Spinelli (Eds.), *School discourse problems* (pp. 231–255). San Diego, CA: College-Hill Press.

Benjamin, H. (1939). *The saber-tooth curriculum.* New York: McGraw-Hill.

Biklen, D. (1990). Communication unbound: Autism and praxis. *Harvard Educational Review, 60,* 291–314.

Blank, M. (1983). *Teaching learning in the preschool: A dialogue approach.* Cambridge, MA: Brookline Books.

Blank, M., Rose, S., & Berlin, L. (1978). *The language of learning: The preschool years.* Orlando, FL: Grune & Stratton.

Bloom, L. (1970). *Language development: Form and function in emerging grammars.* Cambridge, MA: The MIT Press.

Bloom, L., Beckwith, R., & Capatides, J. (1988). Developments in the expression of affect. *Infant Behavior and Development, 11,* 169–186.

Bloom, L., & Capatides, J. (1987). Expression of affect and the emergence of language. *Child Development, 58,* 1513–1522.

Bloom, L., & Lahey, M. (1978). *Language development and language disorders.* New York: John Wiley.

Brewer, W., & Lichtenstein, E. (1982). Stories are to entertain: A structural-affect theory of stories. *Journal of Pragmatics, 6,* 473–486.

Bricker, D. (1993). Then, now, and the path between: A brief history of language intervention. In A. Kaiser & D. Gray (Eds.), *Enhancing children's communication* (pp. 4–31). Baltimore, MD: Paul H. Brookes.

Bricker, D., & Cripe, J. (1992). *An activity-based approach to early intervention.* Baltimore, MD: Paul H. Brookes.

Bricker, W., & Bricker, D. (1974). An early language training strategy. In R. Schiefelbusch & L. Lloyd (Eds.), *Language perspectives: Acquisition, retardation, and intervention* (pp. 431–468). Baltimore, MD: University Park Press.

Brinton, B., & Fujiki, M. (1989). *Conversational management with language-impaired children: Pragmatic assessment and intervention.* Rockville, MD: Aspen

Brinton, B., & Fujiki, M. (1994). Ways to teach conversation. In J. Duchan, L. Hewitt, & R. Sonnenmeier (Eds.), *Pragmatics: From theory to practice* (pp. 59–71). Englewood Cliffs, NJ: Prentice-Hall.

Brown, A., & Ferrara, R. (1985). Diagnosing zones of proximal development. In J. Wertsch (Ed.), *Culture, communication, and cognition: Vygotskian perspectives* (pp. 273–305). New York: Cambridge University Press.

Brown, R. (1973). *A first language: The early stages.* Cambridge, MA: Harvard University Press.

Bruder, G. (in press). Psychological testing of temporal and spatial components of the deictic center theory. In J. Duchan, G. Bruder, & L. Hewitt (Eds.), *Deixis in narrative: A cognitive science perspective.* Hillsdale, NJ: Lawrence Erlbaum.

Bruner, J. (1977). Early social interaction and language acquisition. In H. Schaffer (Ed.), *Studies in mother-child interaction* (pp. 271–289). New York: Academic Press.

Bruner, J., & Sherwood, V. (1976). Early rule structure: The case of peekaboo. In

R. Harré (Ed.), *Life sentences: Aspects of the social role of language* (pp. 55–62). New York: John Wiley.

Buttrill, J., Niizawa, J., Biemer, C., Takahashi, C., & Hearn, S. (1989). Serving the language learning disabled adolescent: A strategies-based model. *Language, Speech and Hearing Services in Schools, 20,* 185–204.

Calculator, S. (1986). Promoting the acquisition and generalization of conversational skills by individuals with severe disabilities. *Augmentative and Alternative Communication, 4,* 94–103.

Calculator, S. (1988). Promoting the acquisition and generalization of conversational skills by individuals with severe disabilities. *Augmentative and Alternative Communication, 4,* 94–103.

Calculator, S., & Jorgensen, C. (1991). Integrating AAC instruction into regular education settings: Expounding on best practices. *Augmentative and Alternative Communication, 7,* 204–214.

Cazden, C. (1965). *Environmental assistance to the child's acquisition of grammar.* Unpublished doctoral dissertation, Harvard University, Cambridge, MA.

Cazden, C. (1979). Peekaboo as an instructional model: Discourse development at home and at school. *Papers and Reports on Child Language Development, 17,* 1–29.

Cazden, C. (1988). *Classroom discourse.* Portsmouth, NH: Heinemann.

Chapman, R. (1981). Exploring children's communicative intents. In J. Miller (Ed.), *Assessing language production in children* (pp. 111–136). Baltimore, MD: University Park Press.

Charlesworth, R., & Hartup, W. (1967). Positive social reinforcement in the nursery school peer group. *Child Development, 38,* 993–1002.

Chomsky, N. (1965). *Aspects of the theory of syntax.* Cambridge, MA: MIT Press.

Clifford, J. (1988). On ethnographic self-fashioning: Conrad and Malinowski. In J. Clifford (Ed.), *The predicament of culture* (pp. 92–113). Cambridge, MA: Harvard University Press.

Cole, K., & Dale, P. (1986). Direct language instruction and interactive language instruction with language delayed preschool children: A comparison study. *Journal of Speech and Hearing Research, 29,* 206–217.

Connell, P. (1982). On training language rules. *Language, Speech and Hearing Services in Schools, 13,* 231–240.

Constable, C. (1983). Creating communicative contexts. In H. Winitz (Ed.), *Language disorders: For clinicians, by clinicians* (pp. 97–120). Baltimore, MD: University Park Press.

Constable, C. (1986). The application of scripts in the organization of language intervention. In K. Nelson (Ed.), *Event knowledge* (pp. 205–230). Hillsdale, NJ: Lawrence Erlbaum.

Crago, M. (1988). *Cultural context in the communicative interaction of young Inuit children.* Unpublished doctoral dissertation, McGill University, Montreal, Quebec.

Crago, M., & Eriks-Brophy, S. (1994). Culture, conversation and interaction: Implications for intervention. In J. Duchan, L. Hewitt, & R. Sonnenmeier (Eds.), *Pragmatics: From theory to practice* (pp. 43–58). Englewood Cliffs, NJ: Prentice-Hall.

Creaghead, N. (1992). *Classroom language intervention: Developing schema for school success.* Buffalo, NY: Educom Associates.

Cremin, L. (1959). John Dewey and the progressive education movement. *School Review, 67,* 160–171.

Cross, T. (1978). Mother's speech and its association with rate of linguistic development in young children. In N. Waterson & C. Snow (Eds.), *The development of communication.* New York: John Wiley.

Crossley, R., & MacDonald, A. (1980). *Annie's coming out.* New York: Penguin.

Crystal, D. (1987). Teaching vocabulary: The case for a semantic curriculum. *Child Language Teaching and Therapy, 3,* 40–56.

Culatta, B. (1984). A discourse based approach to training grammatical rules. *Seminars in Speech and Language, 5,* 253–263.

Culatta, B. (1994). Representational play and story enactments: Formats for language intervention. In J. Duchan, L. Hewitt, & R. Sonnenmeier (Eds.), *Pragmatics: From theory to practice* (pp. 105–119). Englewood Cliffs, NJ: Prentice-Hall.

Culatta, B., & Horn, D. (1982). A program for achieving generalization of grammatical rules to spontaneous discourse. *Journal of Speech and Hearing Disorders, 47,* 174–181.

de Laguna, G. (1963). *Speech: Its function and development.* Bloomington: Indiana University Press. (Original work published in 1927)

DePaepe, P., Reichle, J., & O'Neill, R. (1993). Applying general-case instructional strategies when teaching communicative alternatives to challenging behavior. In J. Reichele & D. Wacker (Eds.), *Communicative alternatives to challenging behavior* (pp. 237–262). Baltimore, MD: Paul H. Brookes.

Dewey, J. (1903). *The child and the curriculum.* Chicago, IL: University of Chicago Press.

Dewey, J. (1938). *Experience and education.* New York: Macmillan.

Dewey, J. (1976). The university elementary school. In A. Boydston (Ed.), *J. Dewey: Essays on school and society, 1899–1901* (pp. 317–320). Carbondale: Southern Illinois University Press.

Dollaghan, C., & Kaston, N. (1986). A comprehension monitoring program for language-impaired children. *Journal of Speech and Hearing Disorders, 51,* 264–271.

Domingo, R. (in press). Adults with mental retardation in an instructional context. In R. Bloom, L. Obler, S. De Santi, & J. Ehrlich (Eds.), *Discourse studies in adult clinical populations.* Hillsdale, NJ: Lawrence Erlbaum.

Donahue, M. (1984). Learning disabled children's conversational competence: An attempt to activate an inactive listener. *Applied Psycholinguistics, 5,* 21–36.

Donnellan, A., Mirenda, P., Mesaros, R., & Fassbender, L. (1984). Analyzing the communicative functions of aberrant behavior. *Journal of the Association for Persons with Severe Handicaps, 9,* 201–212.

Dore, J. (1975). Holophrases, speech acts, and language universals. *Journal of Child Language, 2,* 21–40.

Duchan, J. (1983). Autistic children are noninteractive: Or so we say. *Seminars in Speech and Language, 4,* 53–61.

Duchan, J. (1984). Language assessment: The pragmatics revolution. In R. Naremore (Ed.), *Language sciences* (pp. 147–180). San Diego, CA: College-Hill Press.

Duchan, J. (1986). Language intervention through sensemaking and fine tuning. In R. Schiefelbusch (Ed.), *Language competence: Assessment and intervention* (pp. 182–212). San Diego, CA: College-Hill Press.

Duchan, J. (1987). Functionalism: A perspective on autistic communication. In D. Cohen & A. Donnellan (Eds.), *Handbook of autism and pervasive developmental disorders* (pp. 703–709). New York: John Wiley.

Duchan, J. (1991). Everyday events: Their role in language assessment and intervention. In T. Gallagher (Ed.), *Pragmatics of language: Clinical practice issues* (pp. 43–98). San Diego, CA: Singular Publishing Group.

Duchan, J. (1993a). *Ethnographic implications of IRE instructional sequence.* Paper presented at the Ethnography Conference, Urbana, IL.

Duchan, J. (1993b). Issues raised by facilitated communication for theorizing and research on autism. *Journal of Speech and Hearing Research, 36,* 1108–1119.

Duchan, J. (1994a). *Dancing together: A new metaphor for understanding facilitated communication.* Unpublished manuscript.

Duchan, J. (1994b). Intervention principles for gestalt-style learners. In J. Duchan, L. Hewitt, & R. Sonnenmeier (Eds.), *Pragmatics: From theory to practice* (pp. 149–163). Hillsdale, NJ: Prentice-Hall.

Duchan, J. (in press). Preschool children's introduction of characters into their oral stories — Evidence for deictic organization of first narratives. In J. Duchan, G. Bruder, & L. Hewitt (Eds.), *Deixis in narrative: A cognitive science perspective.* Hillsdale, NJ: Lawrence Erlbaum.

Duchan, J., Bruder, G., & Hewitt, L. (Eds.). (in press). *Deixis in narrative: A cognitive science perspective.* Hillsdale, NJ: Lawrence Erlbaum.

Duchan, J., Hewitt, L., & Sonnenmeier, R. (1994). *Pragmatics: From theory to practice.* Englewood Cliffs, NJ: Prentice-Hall.

Duchan, J., Meth, M., & Waltzman, D. (1992). "Then" as an indicator of deictic discontinuity in adults' descriptions of a film. *Journal of Speech and Hearing Research, 35,* 1367–1375.

Duchan, J., & Weitzner-Lin, B. (1987). Nurturant-naturalistic language intervention for language impaired children: Implications for planning lessons and tracking progress. *Asha, 29,* 45–49.

Dunst, C., Trivette, C., & Deal, A. (1988). *Enabling and empowering families.* Cambridge, MA: Brookline Books.

Edelsky, C., Altwerger, B., & Flores, B. (1991). *Whole language: What's the difference?* Portsmouth, NH: Heinemann Educational Books.

Eder, D. (1982). Differences in communicative styles across ability groups. In L. Wilkinson, (Ed.), *Communicating in the classroom* (pp. 245–264). New York: Academic Press.

Educational Productions, Inc. (1987). *Let's talk: First steps to conversation.* [Video training program]. Portland OR: Author.

Educational Productions, Inc. (1988). *Space to grow: Creating an enviroment that supports language acquisition.* [Video training program]. Portland, OR: Author.

Eriks-Brophy A., & Crago, M. (1993). Inuit efforts to maintain face: Elements from classroom discourse with Inuit children. In D. Kovarsky, M. Maxwell, & J. Damico (Eds.), *Language interaction in clinical and educational settings,* ASHA Monographs No. 30 (pp. 10–16). Rockville, MD: American Speech-Language-Hearing Association.

Esterreicher, C. (1992/1993, Winter). Magic, JARS. *Clinical Connection,* pp. 20–22.

Evans, M. (1987). Discourse characteristics of reticent children. *Applied Psycholinguistics, 8,* 171–184.

Ezell, H., & Goldstein, H. (1991). Observational learning of comprehension monitoring skills in children who exhibit mental retardation. *Journal of Speech and Hearing Research, 34,* 141–154.

Farrar, D., & Goodman, G. (1992). Developmental changes in event memory. *Child Development, 63,* 173–187.

Felson-Rubin, N. (1992). *Bakhtinian alterity, Homeric rapport.* Unpublished manuscript.

Ferguson, C. (1979). Phonology as an individual access system: Some data from language acquisition. In C. Fillmore, D. Kempler, & W. S-Y. Wang (Eds.), *Individual differences in language ability and language behavior* (pp. 189–201). New York: Academic Press.

Fey, M. (1986). *Language intervention with young children.* San Diego, CA: College-Hill Press.

Fillmore, L. (1989). Individual differences in second language acquisition. In C. Fillmore, D. Kempler, & W. S-Y. Wang (Eds.), *Individual differences in language ability and language behavior* (pp. 203–228). New York: Academic Press.

Fishman, P. (1978). Interaction: The work women do. *Social Problems, 25,* 397–406.

Flaherty, C. (1993). Gaining group cooperation through role playing. *Child Language Teaching and Therapy, 9,* 32–44.

Fletcher, P. (1983). An outsider's view of language intervention. In J. Miller, D. Yoder, & R. Schiefelbusch (Eds.), *Contemporary issues in language intervention* (pp. 326–330). Rockville, MD: The American Speech-Language-Hearing Association.

Fokes, J. (1976). *Fokes sentence builder.* Boston, MA: Teaching Resources.

Forest, M., & Pearpoint, J. (1992). Families, friends, and circles. In J. Nisbet (Ed.), *Natural supports in school, at work, and in the community for people with severe disabilities* (pp. 65–86). Baltimore, MD: Paul H. Brookes.

Friedman, P., & Friedman, K. (1980). Accounting for individual differences when comparing the effectiveness of remedial language teaching methods. *Applied Psycholinguistics, 1,* 151–170.

Gallagher, T., & Craig, H. (1984). Pragmatic assessment: Analysis of a highly frequent repeated utterance. *Journal of Speech and Hearing Disorders, 49,* 368–377.

Gallagher, T., & Darnton, B. (1978). Conversational aspects of the speech of language-disordered children: Revision behaviors. *Journal of Speech and Hearing Research, 21,* 118–135.

Geertz, C. (1973a). *The interpretation of cultures.* New York: Basic Books.

Geertz, C. (1973b). Thick description: Toward an interpretive theory of culture. In C. Geertz (Ed.), *The interpretation of cultures* (pp. 3–30). New York: Basic Books.

Gillham, W. (1979). *The first words language programme: A basic language programme for mentally handicapped children.* London: Allen & Unwin.

Gillham, W. (1990). First words in normal and Down syndrome children: A Comparison of content and word-form categories. *Child Language Teaching and Therapy, 6,* 25–32.

Goffman, E. (1961). *Encounters: Two studies in the sociology of interaction.* New York: Bobbs-Merrill.

Goffman, E. (1974). *Frame analysis*. New York: Harper & Row.

Goldstein, H., & Gallagher, T. (1992). Strategies for promoting the social communicative competence of young children with specific language impairment. In S. Odom, S. O'Connell, & M. McEvoy (Eds.), *Social competence of young children with disabilities* (pp. 189–213). Baltimore, MD: Paul H. Brookes.

Goldstein, H., Wickstrom, S., Hoyson, M., Jamieson, B., & Odom, S. (1988), Effects of sociodramatic play training on social and communicative interaction. *Education and Treatment of Children, 11*, 97–117.

Goode, D. (1979). The world of the congenitally deaf-blind: Toward the grounds for achieving human understanding. In J. Jacobs & H. Schwartz (Eds.), *Qualitative sociology* (pp. 381–396). New York: Free Press.

Goode, D. (1992). Who is Bobby? Ideology and method in the discovery of a Down syndrome person's competence. In P. Ferguson, D. Ferguson, & S. Taylor (Eds.). *Interpreting disability: A qualitative reader* (pp. 197–212). New York: Teachers College Press.

Goodman, G. Duchan, J., & Sonnenmeier, R. (1994). Children's development of scriptal knowledge. In J. Duchan, L. Hewitt, & R. Sonnenmeier (Eds.), *Pragmatics: From theory to practice* (pp. 120–133). Englewood Cliffs, NJ: Prentice-Hall.

Goodman, K. (1986). *What's whole in whole language?* Portsmouth, NH: Heinemann Educational Books.

Goodwin, M. (1990) *He-said-she-said*. Bloomington: Indiana University Press.

Gopnik, A. (1982). Words and plans: Early language and the development of intelligent action. *Journal of Child Language, 9*, 303–318.

Gray, B., & Fygetakis, L. (1968). Mediated language acquisition for dysphasic children. *Behavioral Research and Therapy, 6*, 263–280.

Gray, B., & Ryan, B. (1973). *A language program for the non-language child*. Champaign, IL: Research Press.

Guess, D., Sailor, W., & Baer, D. (1974). To teach language to retarded children In R. Schiefelbusch & L. Lloyd (Eds.), *Language perspectives: Acquisition, retardation, and intervention* (pp. 529–536). Baltimore, MD: University Park Press.

Guess, D., Sailor, W., Rutherford, G., & Baer, D. (1968). An experimental analysis of linguistic development: The productive use of the plural morpheme. *Journal of Applied Behavioral Analysis, 1*, 297–306.

Halliday, M. (1975). *Learning how to mean: Explorations in the development of language*. London: Edward Arnold.

Halliday, M., & Hasan, R. (1976). *Cohesion in English*. New York: Longman.

Haring, T. (1992). The context of social competence: Relations, relationships and generalization. In S. Odom, S. O'Connell, & M. McEvoy (Eds.), *Social competence of young children with disabilities* (pp. 307–320), Baltimore, MD: Paul H. Brookes.

Haring, T., & Lovinger, L. (1989). Promoting social interaction through teaching generalized play initiation responses to preschool children with autism. *Journal of The Association for Persons with Severe Handicaps, 14*, 58–67.

Harris, K. (1990). Meeting diverse needs through collaborative consultation. In W. Stainback & S. Stainback (Eds.), *Support networks for inclusive schooling* (pp. 139–150). Baltimore, MD: Paul H. Brookes.

Hart, B., & Risley, T. (1968). Establishing the use of descriptive adjectives in the spontaneous speech of disadvantaged preschool children. *Journal of Applied Behavioral Analysis, 1*, 109–120.

Hart, B., & Rogers-Warren, A. (1978). A milieu approach to teaching language. In R. Schiefelbusch (Ed.), *Language intervention strategies* (pp. 193–235). Baltimore, MD: University Park Press.

Heath, S. (1982). What no bedtime story means: Narrative skills at home and school. *Language in Society, 11,* 49–76.

Heath, S. (1983). *Ways with words: Language, life and work in communities and classrooms.* New York: Cambridge University Press.

Heath, S. (1986). Sociocultural contexts of language development. In Bilingual Education Office, California State Department of Education (Eds.), *Beyond language: Social and cultural factors in schooling language minority students* (pp. 146–186). Los Angeles, CA: Evaluation, Dissemination and Assessment Center, California State University.

Heath, S., & Branscombe, A. (1986). The book as narrative prop in language acquisition. In B. Schieffelin & P. Gilmore (Eds.), *Advances in discourse processes: Vol. 11. The acquisition of literacy: Ethnographic perspectives* (pp. 16–34). Norwood, NJ: Ablex.

Hegde, M. (1980). An experimental-clinical analysis of grammatical and behavioral distinctions between verbal auxiliary and copula. *Journal of Speech and Hearing Research, 23,* 864–877.

Hegde, M., & Gierut, J. (1979). The operant training and generalization of pronouns and a verb form in a language delayed child. *Journal of Communication Disorders, 12,* 23–34.

Hewitt, L. (1994). Facilitating narrative comprehension: The importance of subjectivity. In J. Duchan, L. Hewitt, & R. Sonnenmeier (Eds.), *Pragmatics: From theory to practice* (pp. 88–104). Englewood Cliffs, NJ: Prentice-Hall.

Hewitt, L., & Duchan, J. (in press). Subjectivity in children's fictional narratives. *Topics in Language Disorders.*

Hill, S., & Hill, T. (1990). *The collaborative classroom.* Portsmouth, NH: Heinemann.

Hinds, J. (1983). Contrastive rhetoric: Japanese and English. *Text, 3,* 183–196.

Hood, L., McDermott, R., & Cole, M. (1980). "Let's try to make it a good day" — Some not so simple ways. *Discourse Processes, 3,* 155–168.

Hymes, D. (1972). Toward ethnographies of communication: The analysis of communicative events. In P. Giglio (Ed.), *Language and social context* (pp. 21–44). Harmondsworth, England: Penguin.

Idol, L., Paolucci-Whitcomb, P., & Nevin, A. (1986). *Collaborative consultation.* Rockville, MD: Aspen.

James, W. (1890). *The principles of psychology.* New York: Henry Holt.

James, W. (1958). *Talks to teachers.* New York: W. W. Norton.

James, W. (1962). *Psychology* (Briefer course). New York: Crowell Collier.

Jeffree, C., Wheldall, K., & Mittler, P. (1973). Facilitating two-word utterances in two Down's syndrome boys. *American Journal of Mental Deficiency, 78,* 117–122.

Johnson, D., & Johnson, R. (1987). *Structuring co-operative learning.* Edina, MN: Interaction Book Co.

Johnston, J. (1985). Fit, focus and functionality: An essay on early language intervention. *Child Language Teaching and Therapy, 1,* 125–134.

Johnston, S., & Reichle, J. (1993). Designing and implementing interventions to decrease challenging behavior. *Language Speech and Hearing Services in Schools, 23,* 225–235.

Jorgensen, C. (1992). Natural supports in inclusive schools. In J. Nisbet (Ed.), *Natural supports in school, at work, and in the community for people with severe disabilities* (pp. 179–215), Baltimore, MD: Paul H. Brookes.

Kanner, L. (1943). Autistic disturbances of affective contact. *Nervous Child, 2,* 217–250.

Kant, I (1787/1965). *Critique of pure reason.* (N. Smith, trans.). New York: St. Martin's Press.

Kaye, K., & Charney, R. (1981). Conversational asymmetry between mothers and children. *Journal of Child Language, 8,* 35–50.

Kent, L. (1974). *Language acquisition program for the retarded or multiply impaired.* Champaign, IL: Research Press.

Kirchner, D. (1991a). Reciprocal book reading: A discourse-based intervention strategy for the child with atypical language development. In T. Gallagher (Ed.), *Pragmatics of language: Clinical practice issues* (pp. 307–332). San Diego: Singular Publishing Group.

Kirchner, D. (1991b). Using verbal scaffolding to facilitate conversational participation and language acquisition in children with pervasive developmental disorders. *Journal of Childhood Communication Disorders, 14,* 81–96.

Klecan-Aker, J. (1993). A treatment programme for improving story-telling ability: A case study. *Child Language Teaching and Therapy, 9,* 105–115.

Kovarsky, D., & Duchan, J. (1992). *The discourse of child and adult centered language intervention.* Paper presented at the First Ethnography Conference, Urbana, IL.

Kuper, A. (1983). *Anthropology and anthropologists: The modern British school* (2nd ed.). New York: Routledge & Kegan Paul.

Lahey, M. (1988). *Language disorders and language development.* New York: Macmillan.

Lakoff, G. (1987). *Women, fire, and dangerous things.* Chicago, IL: University of Chicago Press.

Lave, J., & Wegner, E. (1991). *Situated learning: Legitimate peripheral participation.* New York: Cambridge University Press.

Lee, L., Koenigsknecht, R., & Mulhern, S. (1975). *Interactive language development teaching.* Evanston, IL: Northwestern University Press.

Leonard, L. (1975). Relational meaning and the facilitation of slow-learning children's language. *American Journal of Mental Deficiency, 80,* 180–185.

Leonard, L. (1981). Facilitating linguistic skills in children with specific language impairment. *Applied Psycholinguistics, 2,* 89–118.

Leonard, L., & Fey, M. (1991). Facilitating grammatical development: The contribution of pragmatics. In T. Gallagher (Ed.), *Pragmatics of language: Clinical practice issues* (pp. 333–355). San Diego, CA: Singular Publishing Group.

Lieberman, J., & Michael, A. (1986). Group therapy revisited: Using cooperative learning procedures in speech-language therapy. *NSSLHA Journal, 14,* 51–67.

Lovaas, O. (1968). A program for the establishment of speech in psychotic children. In H. Sloane & B. MacAuley (Eds.), *Operant procedures in remedial speech and language training* (pp. 125–154). New York: Houghton Mifflin.

Lovaas, O., Berberich, J., Perloff, B., & Schaeffer, B. (1966). Acquisition of imitative speech by schizophrenic children. *Science, 151,* 705–707.

Loveland, K., & Tunali, B. (1991). Social scripts for conversational interactions in autism and Down syndrome. *Journal of Autism and Developmental Disorders, 21,* 177–186.

Lund, N., & Duchan, J. (1987, April). *What happened in school today?* Miniseminar presented to New York State Speech, Language and Hearing Association Convention, Monticello.

Lund, N., & Duchan, J. (1993). *Assessing children's language in naturalistic contexts* (3rd ed.). Englewood Cliffs, NJ: Prentice-Hall.

Lynch, E., & Hanson, M. (1992). *Developing cross-cultural competence: A guide for working with young children and their families.* Baltimore, MD: Paul H. Brookes.

MacDonald, J., Blott, J., Gordon, K., Spiegel, B., & Hartmann, M. (1974). An experimental parent-assisted treatment program for preschool language-delayed children. *Journal of Speech and Hearing Disorders, 39,* 395–415.

Mackan, P., & Cormier, R. (1992). The dynamics of support circles. In J. Pearpoint, M. Forest, & J. Snow (Eds), *The inclusion papers: Strategies to make inclusion work* (pp. 58–61). Toronto, Ontario: The Inclusion Press.

MacKay, R. (1974). Standardized tests: Objective/objectified measures of "competence." In A. Cicourel, K. Jennings, S. Jennings, K. Leiter, R. Mackay, H. Mehan, & D. Roth (Eds.), *Language use and school performance* (pp. 218–247). New York: Academic Press.

Malinowski, B. (1922). *Argonauts of the Western Pacific.* London: Routlege.

Manning, A., & Katz, K. (1989). Language-learning patterns in echolalic children. *Child Language Teaching and Therapy, 5,* 249–261.

Masters, J., & Pine, S. (1992). Incidental group language therapy: Verbal and preverbal children. *Child Language Teaching and Therapy, 8,* 18–29.

McEvoy, M., Odom, S., & McConnell, S. (1992). Peer social competence intervention for young children with disabilities. In S. Odom, S. McConnell, & M. McEvoy (Eds.), *Social competence of young children with disabilities* (pp. 113–133). Baltimore, MD: Paul H. Brookes.

McEvoy, M., Twardosz, S., & Bishop, N. (1990). Affection activities: Procedures for encouraging young children with handicaps to interact with their peers. *Education and Treatment of Children, 13,* 159–167.

McShane, J. (1980). *Learning to talk.* New York: Cambridge University Press.

McTear, M., & Conti-Ramsden, G. (1992). *Pragmatic disability in children.* San Diego, CA: Singular Publishing Group.

Mead, G. H. (1932). The objective reality of perspectives. In G. H. Mead, *The philosophy of the present.* Chicago, IL: University of Chicago Press.

Mead, G. H. (1934). *Mind, self and society: From the standpoint of a social behaviorist.* Chicago, IL: University of Chicago Press.

Mehan, H. (1979). *Learning lessons: Social organization in the classroom.* Cambridge, MA: Harvard University Press.

Merritt, M. (1982). Distributing and directing attention in primary classrooms. In L. Wilkinson (Ed.), *Communicating in the classroom* (pp. 223–244). New York: Academic Press.

Michaels, S. (1981). "Sharing time": Children's narrative style and differential access to literacy. *Language in Society, 10,* 423–442.

Michaels, S. (1986). Narrative presentations: An oral preparation for literacy with first graders. In J. Cook-Gumperz (Ed.), *The social construction of literacy* (pp. 94–116). New York: Cambridge University Press.

Michaels, S., & Cazden, C. (1986). Teacher/child collaboration as oral preparation for literacy. In B. Schieffelin & P. Gilmore (Eds.), *The acquisition of literacy: Ethnographic perspectives* (pp. 132–154). Norwood, NJ: Ablex.

Miller, A., & Eller-Miller, E. (1989). *From ritual to repertoire.* New York: John Wiley.

Miller, A., & Miller E. (1973). Cognitive developmental training with elevated boards and sign language. *Journal of Autism and Childhood Schizophrenia, 3,* 65–85.

Miller, J., & Yoder, D. (1974). An ontogenetic language teaching strategy for retarded children. In R. Schiefelbusch & L. Lloyd (Eds.), *Language perspectives: Acquisition, retardation and intervention* (pp. 505–528). Baltimore, MD: University Park Press.

Miller, L. (1989). Classroom-based language intervention. *Language, Speech and Hearing Services in Schools, 20,* 153–169.

Miller, P. (1986). Teasing as language socialization and verbal play in a white working class community. In B. Schieffelin & E. Ochs (Eds.), *Language socialization across cultures* (pp. 199–212). New York: Cambridge University Press.

Miller, P., & Sperry, L. (1988). Early talk about the past: The origins of conversational stories of personal experience. *Journal of Child Language, 15,* 293–315.

Moll, L. (1992). *Vygotsky and education: Instructional implications and applications of sociohistorical psychology.* New York: Cambridge University Press.

Morris, C. (1970). *The pragmatic movement in American philosophy.* New York: George Braziller.

Mulac, A., & Tomlinson, C. (1977). Generalization of an operant remediation program for syntax with language delayed children. *Journal of Communication Disorders, 10,* 231–243.

Neitupski, J., Hamre-Neitupski, S., Clancy, P., & Veerhusen, K. (1986). Guidelines for making simulation an effective adjunct to in vivo community instruction. *The Journal of the Association for Persons with Severe Handicaps, 11,* 12–18.

Nelson, K. (1973). Structure and strategy in learning to talk. *Society for Research in Child Development Monographs, 38*(1/2, Serial No. 149).

Nelson, K. (1985). *Making sense: The acquisition of shared meaning.* New York: Academic Press.

Nelson, K. (1986). *Event knowledge, structure, and function in development.* Hillsdale, NJ: Lawrence Erlbaum.

Nelson, K. (1991a). Concepts and meaning in language development. In N. Krasnegor, D. Rumbaugh, R. Schiefelbusch, & M. Studdert-Kennedy (Eds.), *Biological and behavioral determinants of language development* (pp. 89–115). Hillsdale, NJ: Lawrence Erlbaum.

Nelson, K. (1991b). Event knowledge and the development of language functions. In J. Miller (Ed.), *Research on child language disorders: A decade of progress* (pp. 125–141). Austin, TX: Pro-Ed.

Nelson, K., & Gruendel, J. (1981). Generalized event representations: Basic building blocks of cognitive development. In M. Lamb & A. Brown (Eds.), *Advances in developmental psychology* (pp. 131–158). Hillsdale, NJ: Lawrence Erlbaum.

Nelson, N. (1989). Curriculum-based language assessment and intervention. *Language, Speech and Hearing Services in Schools, 20,* 170–184.

Nelson, N. (1993). *Childhood language disorders in context.* New York: Macmillan.

Nodelman, P. (1988). *Words about pictures: The narrative art of children's picture books.* Athens: The University of Georgia.

Norris, J. (1989). Providing language remediation in the classroom: An integrated language-to-reading intervention method. *Language, Speech and Hearing Services in Schools, 20,* 205–218.

Norris, J., & Damico, J. (1990). Whole language in theory and practice: Implications for language intervention. *Language, Speech and Hearing Services in Schools, 21,* 212–220.

Norris, J., & Hoffman, P. (1990). Comparison of adult-initiated vs. child-initiated interaction styles with handicapped prelanguage children. *Language, Speech and Hearing Services in Schools, 21,* 28–36.

Norris, J., & Hoffman, P. (1993a). *Whole language intervention for school-age children.* San Diego, CA: Singular Publishing Group.

Norris, J., & Hoffman, P. (1993b). Whole language is truly whole. *Newsletter of Special Interest Division 10 of ASHA, 3,* 9–11.

Oates, J. (1987). *On boxing.* New York: Doubleday.

Ochs, E. (1988). *Culture and language development.* New York: Cambridge University Press.

Odom, S., Hoyson, M., Jamieson, B., & Strain, P. (1985). Increasing handicapped preschoolers-peer social interactions: Cross setting and component analysis. *Journal of Applied Behavior Analysis, 18,* 3–16.

Odom, S., Peterson, C., McConnell, S., & Ostrosky, M. (1990). Ecobehavioral analysis of classroom settings that support peer social interaction of young children with and without disabilities. *Education and Treatment of Children, 13,* 274–287.

Odom, S., & Strain, P. (1984). Peer-mediated approaches for promoting children's social interaction: A review. *American Journal of Orthopsychiatry, 54,* 544–557.

Olswang, L., Kriegsmann, E., & Mastergeorge, A. (1982). Facilitating functional requesting in pragmatically impaired children. *Language, Speech and Hearing Services in Schools, 13,* 202–222.

Owens, R. (1991). *Language disorders: A functional approach to assessment and intervention.* New York: Macmillan.

Paley, V. (1981). *Wally's stories: Conversations in the kindergarten.* Cambridge, MA: Harvard University Press.

Paley, V. (1990). *The boy who would be a helicopter.* Boston, MA: Harvard University Press.

Paley, V. (1992). *You can't say you can't play.* Boston, MA: Harvard University Press.

Paley, V. (1994). Every child a storyteller. In J. Duchan, L. Hewitt, & R. Sonnenmeier (Eds.), *Pragmatics from theory to practice* (pp. 10–19). Englewood Cliffs, NJ: Prentice-Hall.

Pearpoint, J. (1991). *From behind the piano: The building of Judith Snow's unique circle of friends.* Toronto: Inclusion Press.

Peirce, C. (1931/1958). *The collected papers of Charles Sanders Peirce* (Vols. 1–6). (C. Hartshorne, P. Weiss, & A. Burks, Eds.). Cambridge, MA: Harvard University Press.

Peters, A. (1983). *The units of language acquisition.* New York: Cambridge University Press.

Peterson, C., & McCabe, A. (1983). *Developmental psycholinguistics: Three ways of looking at a child's narrative.* New York: Plenum.

Philips, S. (1983). *The invisible culture.* New York: Longman.

Piaget, J. (1954). *The construction of reality in the child.* New York: Basic Books.

Pine, J., & Lieven, E. (1993). Reanalysing rote-learned phrases: Individual differences in the transition to multi-word speech. *Journal of Child Language, 20,* 551–572.

Pitcher, E., & Prelinger, E. (1963). *Children tell stories.* New York: International Universities Press.

Porter, R., & Conti-Ramsden, G. (1987). Clarification requests and the language-impaired child. *Child Language Teaching and Therapy, 3,* 133–150.

Prizant, B., & Duchan, J. (1981). The functions of immediate echolalia in autistic children. *Journal of Speech and Hearing Disorders, 46,* 241–249.

Prizant, B., & Rydell, P. (1984). An analysis of the functions of delayed echolalia in autistic children. *Journal of Speech and Hearing Research, 27,* 183–192.

Prizant, B., & Rydell, P. (1993). Assessment and intervention considerations for unconventional verbal behavior. In J. Reichle & D. Wacker (Eds.), *Communicative alternatives to challenging behavior* (pp. 263–297). Baltimore, MD: Paul H. Brookes.

Prizant, B., & Wetherby, A. (1985). Intentional communicative behavior of children with autism: Theoretical and practical issues. *Australian Journal of Human Communication Disorders, 13,* 21–59.

Prutting, C. Bagshaw, N., Goldstein, H., Juskowitz, S., & Umen, I. (1978). Clinician-child discourse: Some preliminary questions. *Journal of Speech and Hearing Disorders, 43,* 123–139.

Ratner, N. & Bruner, J. (1978). Games, social exchange, and the acquisition of language. *Journal of Child Language, 5,* 391–401.

Reddy, M. (1979). The conduit metaphor. In A. Ortony (Ed.), *Metaphor and thought* (pp. 284–324). New York: Cambridge University Press.

Reed, V. (1994). *An introduction to children with language disorders* (2nd ed.). New York: Macmillan.

Reichle, J., Halle, J., & Johnston, S. (1993). Developing an initial communicative repertoire. In A. Kaiser & D. Gray (Eds.), *Enhancing children's communication* (pp. 105–136). Baltimore, MD: Paul H. Brookes.

Reynolds, L. (1993). *Interactionism: Exposition and critique* (3rd ed.). Dix Hills, NY: General Hall.

Rice, M., Wilcox, K., Hadley, P., & Schuele, M. (1993, November). *Facilitating peer interactions: Social skills for preschool and kindergarten success.* Paper presented at the annual convention of the American Speech-Language-Hearing Association, Anaheim, CA.

Ripich, D., & Panagos, J. (1985). Accessing children's knowledge of sociolinguistic rules for speech therapy lessons. *Journal of Speech and Hearing Disorders, 50,* 335–346.

Roth, F., & Spekman, N. (1986). Narrative discourse: Spontaneously generated stories of learning-disabled and normally achieving students. *Journal of Speech and Hearing Disorders, 51,* 8–23.

Rorty, R. (1979). *Philosophy and the mirror of nature.* Princeton, NJ: Princeton University Press.

Rubin, K. (1977). The social and cognitive value of preschool toys and activities. *Canadian Journal of Behavioral Science, 9,* 382–385.

Russell, B. (1905). On denoting. *Mind, 4,* 79–93. Reprinted in B. Russell (1956) *Principles of mathematics* (2nd ed., pp. 41–56). New York: W. W. Norton.

Sachs, J., & Devin, J. (1976). Young children's use of age appropriate speech styles in social interactions and role playing. *Journal of Child Language, 3,* 81–98.

Schank, R. (1982). *Dynamic memory: A theory of learning in computers and people.* New York: Cambridge University Press.

Schank, R., & Ableson, R. (1977). *Scripts, plans, goals and understanding: An inquiry into human knowledge structures.* Hillsdale, NJ: Lawrence Erlbaum.

Schegloff, E. (1968). Sequencing in conversational openings. *American Anthropologist, 70,* 1075–1095.

Scherer, N., & Olswang, L. (1984). Role of mothers' expansions in stimulating children's language production. *Journal of Speech and Hearing Research, 27,* 387–396.

Scherer, N., & Olswang, L. (1989). Using structured discourse as a language intervention technique with autistic children. *Journal of Speech and Hearing Disorders, 54,* 383–394.

Schieffelin, B. (1990). *The give and take of everyday life: Language socialization of Kaluli children.* New York: Cambridge University Press.

Schieffelin, B. (1994). Code-switching and language socialization: Some probable relationships. In J. Duchan, L. Hewitt, & R. Sonnenmeier (Eds.), *Pragmatics: From theory to practice* (pp. 20–42). Englewood Cliffs, NJ: Prentice-Hall.

Schieffelin, B., & Ochs, E. (1986). *Language and socialization across cultures.* New York: Cambridge University Press.

Schiffrin, D. (1987). *Discourse markers.* New York: Cambridge University Press.

Schubert, A. (1992). *Facilitated communication: Resource guide.* Brookline, MA: Adriana Foundation.

Searle, J. (1969). *Speech acts: An essay in the philosophy of language.* New York: Cambridge University Press.

Segal, E. (in press). Introduction to the deictic center. In J. Duchan, G. Bruder, & L. Hewitt (Eds.), *Deixis in narrative: A cognitive science perspective.* Hillsdale, NJ: Lawrence Erlbaum.

Segal, E., Duchan, J., & Scott. P. (1991). The role of interclausal connectives in narrative structuring: Evidence from adults' interpretations of simple stories. *Discourse Processes, 14,* 27–54.

Sharan, Y., & Sharan, S. (1992). *Expanding cooperative learning through group investigation.* New York: Teachers College, Columbia University.

Sherzer, J. (1983). *Kuna ways of speaking.* Austin: University of Texas Press.

Shultz, J. (1979). It's not whether you win or lose, it's how you play the game. In O. Garnica & M. King (Eds.), *Language, children and society* (pp. 271–292). New York: Pergamon Press.

Silliman, E., & Wilkinson, L. (1991). *Communicating for learning. Classroom observation and collaboration.* Gaithersburg, MD: Aspen.

Simon, C. (1980). Communicative competence: Photo diagrams. In C. Simon, *Communicative competence: A functional-pragmatic language program.* Tucson, AZ: Communication Skill Builders.

Simons, J. (1974). Observations on compulsive behavior in autism. *Journal of Autism and Childhood Schizophrenia, 4,* 1–10.

Skarakis-Doyle, E., & Mentis, M. (1991). A discourse approach to language disorders: Investigating complex sentence production. In T. Gallagher (Ed.), *Pragmatics of language: Clinical practice issues* (pp. 283–305). San Diego, CA: Singular Publishing Group.

Skinner, B. (1938). *The behavior of organisms.* New York: Appleton-Century-Crofts.

Slavin, R. (1990). *Cooperative learning: Theory, research, and practice.* Boston: Allyn & Bacon.

Sloane, H., & MacAuley, B. (Eds.). (1968). *Operant procedures in remedial speech and language training.* New York: Houghton Mifflin.

Smilanski, S., & Sheftaya, L. (1990). *Facilitating play.* Gaithersburg, MD: Psychosocial and Educational Publications.

Smith, B., & Leinonen, E. (1992). *Clinical pragmatics: Unravelling the complexities of communicative failure.* New York: Chapman & Hall.

Smith, L. (Ed.). (1987). *Discourse across cultures.* Englewood Cliffs, NJ: Prentice-Hall.

Snow, J., & Forest, M. (1988). *Support circles: Building a vision.* Toronto: Centre for Integrated Education and Community.

Snow, J., & Hasbury, (1989). The circle of friends. In J. O'Brien & M. Forest (Eds.), *Action for inclusion* (pp. 45–46). Toronto, Ontario: Inclusion Press.

Snyder-McLean, L., Solomonson, B., McLean, J., & Sack, S. (1984). Structuring joint action routines: A strategy for facilitating communication and language development in the classroom. *Seminars in Speech and Language, 5,* 213–225.

Sonnenmeier, R. (1993). A longitudinal study of co-construction during facilitated communication. Project proposal for the fulfillment of a requirement for the doctoral degree, University of Buffalo, Buffalo, NY.

Sonnenmeier, R. (1994). Script-based language intervention: Learning to participate in life events. In J. Duchan, L. Hewitt, & R. Sonnenmeier (Eds.), *Pragmatics: From theory to practice* (pp 134–148). Englewood Cliffs, NJ: Prentice-Hall.

Spradley, J. (1979). *The ethnographic interviews.* New York: Holt, Rinehart & Winston.

Spreitzer, E., Snyder, E., & Larson, D. (1979). Multiple roles and psychological well-being. *Sociological Focus, 12,* 141–148.

Stein, N., & Glenn, C. (1979). An analysis of story comprehension in elementary school children. In R. Freedle (Ed.), *New directions in discourse processing* (Vol. 2, pp. 53–120). Norwood, NJ: Ablex.

Stern, D. (1985). *The interpersonal world of the infant.* New York: Basic Books.

Stillman, R., & Battle, C. (1984). Developing prelanguage communication in the severely handicapped: An interpretation of the Van Dijk method. *Seminars in Speech and Language, 5,* 159–170.

Stoneman, Z., Cantrell, M., & Hoover-Dempsey, K. (1983). The association between play materials and social behavior in a mainstreamed preschool: A naturalistic investigation. *Journal of Applied Developmental Psychology, 4,* 163–174.

Stremel-Campbell, K., & Campbell, R. (1985). Training techniques that may facilitate generalization. In S. Warren & A. Rogers-Warren (Eds.), *Teaching functional language.* Baltimore MD: University Park Press.

Stryker, S., & Statham, A. (1985). Symbolic interactionism and role theory. In G. Lindzey & E. Aronson (Eds.), *The handbook of social psychology* (Vol. 1, 3rd ed., pp. 311–378). New York: Random House.

Sugarman, S. (1984). The development of preverbal communication. In R. Schiefelbusch & J. Pikar (Eds.), *The acquisition of communicative competence* (pp. 25–67). Baltimore, MD: University Park Press.

Sutton-Smith, B. (1986). *Toys as culture.* New York: Gardner Press.

Tannen, D. (1980). A comprehensive analysis of oral narrative strategies: Athenian Greek and American English. In W. Chafe (Ed.), *The pear stories* (pp. 51–87). Norwood, NJ: Ablex.

Tannen, D. (1990). *You just don't understand: Women and men in conversation.* New York: William Morrow.

Tharp, R., & Gallimore, R. (1988). *Rousing minds to life.* New York: Cambridge University Press.

Thresher, T. (1992). Facilitated communication at work. *New England Newsletter on Facilitated Communication, 1,* 1.

Todorov, T. (1984). *Mikhail Bakhtin: The dialogical principle.* Minneapolis: University of Minnesota Press.

Tough, J. (1981). *A place for talk.* London, England: Ward Lock Educational in association with Drake Educational Associates.

Twardosz, S., Nordquist, V., Simon, R., & Botkin, D. (1983). The effect of group affection activities on the interaction of socially isolate children. *Analysis and Intervention in Developmental Disabilities, 13,* 311–338.

Van Alstyne, D. (1932). *Play behavior and choice of play materials of preschool children.* Chicago, IL: University of Chicago Press.

van Kleek, A. (1994). Potential cultural bias in training parents as conversational partners with their children who have delays in language development, *American Journal of Speech-Language Pathology, 3,* 67–78.

Van Riper, C. (1963) *Speech correction: Principles and methods* (4th ed.). Englewood Cliffs, NJ: Prentice-Hall.

Vandercook, T., York, J., & Forest, M. (1989). *Strategy for building the vision.* Minneapolis: University of Minnesota, Institute on Community Integration.

Vygotsky, L. (1978). In M. Cole, V. John-Steiner, S. Scribner, & E. Souberman (Eds.), *Mind in society: The development of higher psychological processes.* Cambridge, MA: Harvard University Press.

Walden, T. (1993). Communicating the meaning of events through social referencing. In A. Kaiser & D. Gray (Eds.), *Enhancing children's communication* (pp. 187–199). Baltimore, MD: Paul H. Brookes.

Ward, M. (1971). *Them children: A study in language learning.* Prospect Heights, IL: Waveland Press.

Watson, J. (1914). *Behavior: An introduction to comparative psychology.* New York: Henry Holt.

Watson-Gegeo, K., & Gegeo, D. (1986). Calling out and repeating routines in Kwara'ae children's language socialization. In B. Schieffelin & E. Ochs (Eds.), *Language and socialization across cultures* (pp. 17–50). New York: Cambridge University Press.

Weiner, F., & Ostrowski, A. (1979). Effects of listener uncertainty on articulatory inconsistency. *Journal of Speech and Hearing Disorders, 44,* 487–493.

Weist, R., Wysocka, H., Witkowska-Stadnik, K., Buczowska, E., & Konieczna, E. (1984). The defective tense hypothesis: On the emergence of tense and aspect in child Polish. *Journal of Child Language, 11,* 347–374.

Werner, H., & Kaplan, B. (1963). *Symbol formation: An organismic developmental approach to language and the expression of thought.* New York: John Wiley.

Wertsch, J. (1985a). *Culture, communication, and cognition: Vygotskian perspectives.* New York: Cambridge University Press.

Wertsch, J. (1985b). *Vygotsky and the social formation of mind.* Cambridge, MD: Harvard University Press.

Wertsch, J. (1991). *Voices of the mind.* Cambridge, MA: Harvard University Press.

Westby, C. (1990). Ethnographic interviewing: Asking the right question to the right people in the right ways. *Journal of Childhood Communication Disorders, 13,* 101–111.

Wetherby, A. (1991). Profiling pragmatic abilities in the emerging language of young children. In T. Gallagher (Ed.), *Pragmatics of language: Clinical practice issues* (pp. 249–281). San Diego, CA: Singular Publishing Group.

Wetherby, A., & Prizant, B. (1990). *Communication and Symbolic Behavior Scales* (Research ed.). Chicago, IL: Riverside Publishing.

Wetherby, A., & Prutting, C. (1984). Profiles of communicative and cognitive-social abilities in autistic children. *Journal of Speech and Hearing Research, 27,* 364–377.

White, M. (1955). *The age of analysis.* New York: Houghton Mifflin.

Whitehurst, G., Novak, G., & Zorn, G. (1972). Delayed speech studied in the home. *Developmental Psychology, 7,* 169–177.

Wilkinson, L., & Calculator, S. (1982). Effective speakers: Students' use of language to request and obtain information and action in the classroom. In L. Wilkinson (Ed.), *Communicating in the classroom* (pp. 85–100). New York: Academic Press.

Wilkinson, L., Milosky, L., & Genishi, C. (1986). Second language learners' use of requests and responses in elementary classrooms. *Topics in Language Disorders, 6,* 57–70.

Winnicott, D. (1993). *Talking to parents.* New York: Addison Wesley.

Wood, D., Bruner, J., & Ross, G. (1976). The role of tutoring in problem solving. *Journal of Child Psychology and Psychiatry, 17,* 89–100.

Yoder, P., Kaiser, A., & Alpert, C. (1991). An exploratory study of the interaction between language teaching methods and child characteristics. *Journal of Speech and Hearing Research, 34,* 155–167.

Zweitman, D., & Sonderman, J. (1979). A syntax program designed to present base linguistic structures to language-disordered children. *Journal of Communication Disorders, 12,* 323–337.

Index